CONSPIRACIES OF SILENCE

CAROLINE CHANDLER

A MEMOIR
A SPY STORY

Caroline Chandler
CONSPIRACIES OF SILENCE

Printed and bound in the United States of America.
ISBN: 9781795347082

Cover photo of William Knox Chandler courtesy of the
University of Chicago Photographic Archive, [apf1-01644],
Special Collections Research Center,
University of Chicago Library.

To Knox, the love of my life and my best friend

ACKNOWLEDGMENTS

My endless gratitude goes to Carol Wright, whose consummate editing, literary expertise, inexhaustible patience, and persistence to "get it right" transformed my first draft and its infinite revisions into the finished story. It has been a collaboration in the best sense.

Also, I want to extend my sincere appreciation to my graphic designer, Emily de Rham, whose artful eye and computer ingenuity, as if by magic, set everything onto these pages.

I'm indebted to my four children for their help and support, to the many friends and family members whose interest and encouragement propelled me forward, and to those who read various drafts and revisions along the way. You all know who you are. And finally, my thanks go to Kaaren Janssen and Alan Kaufman, whose help readied the story for publication.

CONTENTS

Part 3

Part 4

PART I

Life can only be understood backwards; but it must be lived forwards.

Søren Kierkegaard, *Journal* (1843)

CHAPTER I
THE FUNERAL

The mourners filed out of the church into the late morning sun. It was mid-July in central Texas, and the ceiling fans had given little relief from the 100-plus temperature during the service. Despite the heat, the men showed their respect by wearing suits and ties and the women by dressing somberly, some of them wearing veiled hats. Outside the church the attendees spoke not so much about their grief as about trivial, comfortable things like the weather: "Hotter than Hades, don't ya think?" and "Can't remember one hotter."

The service celebrated a man's life, a short life by the standards of the mid-20th century, a life that had ended tragically. William Knox Chandler, who would have been my father-in-law had he lived, was 43 years and three months old when he died. He had risen from small-town roots to become a scholar, a teacher at elite universities, and a patriot who served his country in two wars.

Brownwood, where W. K. Chandler would be buried, lay deep in the heart of Texas, about twelve miles from the state's geographical center as the residents often pointed out with great pride. The town also lay within the Bible Belt and its 20,000 inhabitants, mostly Christian and evangelical, were served by 60 or so churches. Some were no more than houses with hand-lettered signs propped in the front windows, the most modest belonging to

Brownwood's black community and located in the black neighborhood, the "Flats." The First Presbyterian Church, however, where the funeral took place, was an imposing brick building that dated back to 1866, only a year after the Civil War. Four massive Doric columns supported its Greek Revival pediment in the front, suggesting permanence and the strong religious faith of the people who climbed the flight of 18 stone steps to worship in the sanctuary every Sunday morning.

By the time the service began, there was standing room only. In the front pews sat Chandlers and Colstons, the families of the deceased. After the other mourners had been seated, Margaret Colston Chandler, the widow, walked down the aisle. She had married W. K. Chandler 14 years earlier in Houston, but the Chandlers had boycotted the wedding because they disapproved of Margaret's parents, who were divorced. Now they were gathered at his funeral. The dead man's parents, Samuel Ezekiel and Carrie Knox Chandler, and his sisters Bettie and Meggs along with their husbands were seated in the front pews. Great aunts and uncles, and cousins once or twice removed on both sides of the family attended, some coming from as far away as San Antonio, South Carolina, and New York. Local friends and neighbors included the town physician, the owner of the local canning company, and a few faculty members and students from Daniel Baker College, which Samuel Ezekiel Chandler had once headed.

My husband Knox[1] sat next to his mother, right in front of the casket. Three months short of his tenth birthday in 1943, Knox was still known by his childhood nickname, "Pachy," which his adoring relatives had bestowed on him when he was an infant. He was sad and uncomfortable, he didn't know how to act, only that he had to be quiet and remain still without fidgeting. For years he would remember sitting beside his weeping mother as the coffin was loaded onto the train that brought his family back from Washington to Texas.

The congregation listened to scripture and sang hymns praising an almighty and merciful God. Some of the mourners may have been disappointed that there had been no viewing of the body, but the Chandlers, shocked as well as grief-stricken, wanted to keep the details of the death as quiet as possible. Although the family was publicly silent about the tragedy, they were well aware that the newspapers had reported the death as a suicide and that in this God-fearing community suicide stood high on the list of mortal sins. The Chandlers would have preferred a private family gathering, but they knew that W. K.'s death would have generated even more speculation if the townspeople had been barred from the service.

---

1 Because this book is about three generations of men named William Knox Chandler, I will refer to my husband's father as W. K. Chandler, my husband as Knox, and our son as Knox Jr. Also for clarity, I have changed Knox's aunt Margaret's name to Meggs and will call my adoptive grandmother, who had many names besides Louise, Lulie.

Friends and relatives got up and eulogized the dead man. Some of his friends and neighbors spoke about his Texas childhood, recalling his love for the out-of-doors and his skill as a hunter and fisherman. Others spoke of his energy and his determination to work tirelessly at whatever he had to do. But the death of such a prominent citizen strained the understanding of those who knew him. Until the day he died, W. K. Chandler's family and even the town had been proud of this man, who had served in World War I, put himself through college, and taught at prestigious universities before he set his professional ambitions aside and agreed to serve his country again in the Second World War. Although the townsfolk knew little of his government work, one of the local papers had reported that it was highly secret, something to do with military strategy. The papers also gave differing accounts of his death. One said that a car accident had been involved; another said that he had died by his own hand.

After the last amen, the congregation gathered on the outskirts of town at Greenleaf Cemetery. The minister intoned the familiar words from Ecclesiastes, "a time to be born, and a time to die... a time of war, and a time of peace." The casket descended into the ground. The mourners embraced one another and shed a few more tears. But my husband, then nine years old, standing in the heat and already bewildered by the church service, understood little of what was said. He could not comprehend why this was the time for his father to die or for his casket to be lowered into a hole in the ground. He only knew what he had been told, that he was now the head of the family, that he must give up his childish nickname, and that he must be brave and strong. His father had left, but Pachy was certain that someday he would return, riding a white horse.

As time passed people seemed to forget the man whose life the funeral celebrated. The war ended; some of Brownwood's war heroes returned to the joy and relief of their families; others lost their lives in the struggle and were memorialized by those who loved them, remembered officially on patriotic holidays and more privately on other days. But a deliberate silence surrounded the memory of W. K. Chandler. Margaret Chandler seldom spoke about her husband and cleared her house of the photos of their life together. The neighbors didn't mention him to his two sons. The circumstances of his death gradually became the Secret. The people who knew what had happened didn't talk about it, or if they did, they spoke in whispers or out of earshot of the boys and Margaret. The Secret remained hidden from his sons for 40 years, creating a silence that would resonate even longer.

Samuel Ezekiel Chandler and Carrie Knox Chandler, 1905

CHAPTER 2
LEAVING TEXAS

W. K. Chandler was born in Kingsville, Texas, on April 12, 1900. He was the middle child and only son of Samuel Ezekiel Chandler and Carrie Knox Chandler, preceded by Elizabeth (Bettie) and followed by Margaret (Meggs). His background was deeply religious. Born in 1861 in South Carolina as the Civil War broke out, Samuel Ezekiel also known as S. E., became a formidable man of God: a scholar of Latin, Greek, and Hebrew and a Doctor of Divinity. Ordained in the Presbyterian Church whose Southern fundamentalist philosophy took a dark view of human nature, S. E. would have believed that man is born in a state of total depravity, that any goodness he might achieve comes from God, and that faith in Jesus Christ is the only route to salvation.

S. E. Chandler served as president of Daniel Baker College in Brownwood, and taught Latin and Greek there and in several other Presbyterian institutions.

At some stage during his tenure, perhaps during difficult financial times, S. E. suffered an episode of what was then called "nerves" and was sent to Asheville, Virginia, for a "rest." Perhaps he had inherited his nerves, his psychological vulnerability, from his father, Ezekiel Chandler, about whom the only thing the family recalls is that he was an alcoholic.

But if S. E. Chandler's nerves were fragile, his expectations were not. His students at Daniel Baker College were required to be diligent in prayer and study and to be mannerly at all times. Still they liked him well enough to call him Uncle Zeke and his wife Aunt Carrie, and his message to the graduating class in the 1934 yearbook suggests warm feelings toward the student body: "With best wishes for all, I am, your friend and fellow-worker. S. E. Chandler."

With his own family he seems to have been more severe, though the household he headed was probably typical of many in the Bible Belt at the beginning of the 20th century. The husband, provider and disciplinarian, ruled the family as the Bible and social convention required. Wives obeyed and served their husbands, managed the housekeeping, cooked the meals, and raised the children. Carrie addressed her husband as "Mr. Chandler" in front of the family, a sign of respect. The rules S. E. imposed, shaped by his fundamentalist beliefs, possibly became even more rigid in reaction to his father's alcoholism; S. E. prohibited smoking, foul language, card games with decks that could also be used for gambling, and, of course, alcohol in any form. On the Sabbath he required his children to attend both Sunday school and church.

An often repeated family story suggests his domineering nature. One Thanksgiving while carving the turkey, S. E. asked his teenage granddaughter Carol whether she wanted dark or white meat. She answered, "It doesn't matter." Her grandfather asked a second and a third time, and each time Carol replied the same way. Infuriated, S. E. sent her to her room without dinner. Her mother, Bettie, afraid to defy her father, remained silent, but later, S. E.'s wife Carrie, avoiding a confrontation, sneaked Carol a plate of dinner. For W. K. this punitive household headed by an emotionally distant father would be the only model he knew as he interacted with his own family, though W. K. would be less distant and less domineering than his father had been.

Until my research turned up the *vita* he wrote when he entered government service, details about W. K. Chandler's life were restricted to things my husband could remember, the few tales his widow would tell about their marriage, and a few academic works that remained within the family. He graduated from Kingsville High School in 1917, toward the end of World War I. Not long after graduation, he enlisted in the army, getting his parents' permission as he was not yet 18. Possibly his enlistment soon after graduation meant that he wanted to get away from Brownwood's small-town fundamentalism and perhaps discover a more adventurous life. Even today, the town numbers only 26,000 with the King Ranch Museum its most important attraction and ballplayer Jim Morris its most famous son.

After the war, when he was 25, W. K. entered the University of Texas in Austin where he earned undergraduate and master's degrees in English, aided surely by his photographic memory. Like his father

W. K. and Margaret, 1929

he studied Greek and Latin, but instead of entering the ministry, he turned to 18th-century literature, the literature of the "Age of Reason." In Austin he met Margaret Colston, also a graduate of the University of Texas, and the two were married in 1929 in Houston.

Margaret's personality seems to have asserted itself early, if one of her stories is any indication. "Your father and I were newlyweds," she later told my husband, with a glimmer of self-satisfaction. "One night he had gotten into bed and I was about to join him when he asked me to turn out the light. I refused. I told him that he had turned it on, that he would just have to get out of bed and turn it off. I was determined to start off on the right foot." From her point of view, she was only asserting what she thought was fair, though her assertiveness bordered on the confrontational.

After W. K. finished his master's degree, the couple headed to the University of Chicago where W. K. showed himself to be remarkably productive. He wrote and defended his PhD thesis on "The Dunciad," a long satirical poem by Alexander Pope. He published an essay on the poetry of Matthew Prior, wrote a student handbook on the mechanics of writing papers, and with his colleague Walter Blair co-authored an anthology of poetry that would go through eleven editions. In addition he managed his teaching duties with the kind of high energy that marked his entire career.

In 1934, a year after my husband Knox was born, the young couple moved to Cambridge where W. K. spent six years as instructor and assistant professor at Harvard, a period that included a sabbatical, where he continued his research in England and Germany. Good-looking and charismatic, W. K. was described by his colleagues as intelligent, focused, and enthusiastically dedicated to his work. His winning sense of humor and his down-home Texas vocabulary made him a popular lecturer at Harvard and Radcliffe. A piece in the *Harvard Crimson* suggests also the affection his students felt for him, as well as his talent as a teacher:

> At two o'clock this afternoon there will descend the steep steps of Sever Hall a strong-jawed, stern-faced figure, dressed picturesquely in chaps, boots, broad sombrero, and all the other paraphernalia of the Western plains. His spurs will catch on the stairs and twirl with a merry ring; his lasso will describe lazy circles over the heads of the admiring assembly. Knox Chandler, the Cowboy Professor, will mount the platform nonchalantly and present his opinions in the most vigorous dialect of the youthful American language. Slang, not the weak, evasive variety, but the short, vibrant phrases, bitten off neatly, inseparably linked with a harsh nasal drawl, and dear to every trans-Mississippi heart, such slang will set, many a pair of ears

W. K. at Radcliffe, 1939

tingling... Come, you vagabonds, come to study the Cowboy Professor. You are guaranteed to hear shrewd perception of literary values which the spontaneous language delightfully accentuates.[1]

At Harvard W. K. continued his academic productivity, writing an essay on James Boswell, Samuel Johnson's great biographer. Entitled "The Discovery of the Boswell Manuscripts," the piece tells a good story with wit and humor, but emphasizes Boswell's personal integrity: "Boswell tells

---

1 "The Vagabond," Harvard Crimson, March 15, 1937; http://www. thecrimson.com/article/1937/3/15/the-vagabond-pat-two-oclock-this/

the truth as he sees it. His apprenticeship to honesty, to truth in his own journals, prepared him to write the greatest of all biographies." A note in Margaret's handwriting accompanying the essay remarks that "he got lots of compliments on this paper, though it was never published."

W. K. made friends at Harvard. Shortly after becoming an instructor he instituted the first departmental Texas-style barbecue, serving up food unfamiliar to New England palates: legs of lamb and pork slowly roasted over wood fires, down-home sides of baked beans and potato salad, lemon pies, and other Southern delights. W. K.'s former colleague, Walter Blair, came in 1937 and enjoyed himself so thoroughly that he exported the idea to Chicago, where it took root. In 1941, after W. K. had moved to Nashville, his Harvard colleagues sent him plane tickets to return for the event, a gesture that touched him deeply, as plane tickets were expensive.

W. K. was an accomplished amateur photographer and owned a Leica, whose expense suggested how serious he was about this hobby. With it he recorded camping trips and sabbaticals in England and Germany, developing the film himself and enlarging the photographs with an apparatus he had made using the camera lens.

In 1940, the Chandler family, which now included a second son, Colston, moved to Nashville, where W. K. became an associate professor at Vanderbilt University. He had already accomplished a great deal, earning the approval of his professors and colleagues wherever he had worked. He expected to continue in the same way at Vanderbilt, publishing articles in scholarly journals and building a reputation in academia. He had accepted the position at Vanderbilt in part because the English department was nationally recognized and in part because the university reputedly encouraged research and original thinking. There is evidence that at the time of his death W. K. had more work in progress although the undated Boswell paper is all that was passed on in the family, and there is no record of his publishing anything after 1935.

Life in Nashville looked promising. The family had found a comfortable three-bedroom house with a small garden and a big back yard, fragrant with honeysuckle. Margaret was settling in and meeting the wives of other professors and the mothers of other third graders. Pachy was shy, but gradually developing friendships with other children. Colston was still at home, closely connected to his mother.

In 1942 W. K. Chandler did not appear to be a likely candidate for the draft. He had served in World War I and was now 42 years old, married, and the father of two young sons, all of which convinced him that he would not be called up. But the age for the draft had been raised to 45, and without W. K.'s, realizing it, his academic credentials—his research skills and his background of work at prestigious universities—made him a prime candidate for the Office of Strategic Services, the government's newly created centralized intelligence agency. His quiet, scholarly life ended abruptly that summer when he was recruited to join the OSS, "tapped on the shoulder," as it was called at the time. His family back in Texas reported that, when he was approached, he turned down his recruiter twice before accepting.

Events moved quickly: W. K. provided the government with references and a *vita* giving an overview of his experience and qualifications (the document I would uncover more than 50 years later). He packed up his family and sent them back to Brownwood to live with his parents. On September 8, 1942, when he headed for Washington, a promising academic career came to an end.

Margaret, Colston, W. K., and Pachy in Nashville, 1941

Back row: Clara May and George Carter
Front row: John and Lulie Hardee, c. 1910

CHAPTER 3
KENTUCKY

In 1943, the year W. K. Chandler died, I was eight years old, living in Louisville, relatively untouched by the war. To outsiders or casual friends our family seemed middle class and pleasantly ordinary. My father, Russell Teague, was a doctor, an easygoing man, comfortable with himself. My mother, Louise Hardee Teague, was more complicated. Her childhood experience with untimely death and broken marriages had awakened resentments and jealousies that would affect me and my brother Rusty as deeply as Knox's father's death affected him. Our family secret was not as dramatic as the one that Margaret Chandler guarded, but it was almost as poisonous.

Around the turn of the 20th century, my mother's father George Carter, a prosperous businessman, died suddenly, leaving his wife Clara May Carter with six children, not much money, and no life insurance. Clara May tried to keep the family together by selling her jewelry and some of the furniture, but soon she realized she could not support all six children. The oldest, Catherine, who was 14 and able to contribute to the household economy, remained with her mother, but the authorities placed the three boys—Calvin, Cecil, and Frazier—in an orphanage and sought adoptive parents for the two cute, red-headed infants, Louise and her identical twin May, then three months old. Clara May's sister Louise (Lulie), 40 years old and recently married to John Hardee, offered to raise the girls, as did Lulie's sister-in-law in Atlanta, Caroline Hardee Godfrey, provided that she could adopt both. But Clara May could not bear giving up both babies, so she let Lulie, who raised both the girls adopt Louise but not May. Louise thus became Louise Hardee, while May remained May Carter. The adoption caused injuries that never healed, my mother Louise always resentful that her mother had given her away and her sister May equally bitter that she had not been adopted. When the girls reached school age, their different last names confused their teachers and classmates, but, worse, permanently reminded Louise and May of their grievances.

When the girls were five, John Hardee died of a heart attack, and Lulie went to work supporting the twins, working as a legal secretary and eking out extra money taking boarders into her Louisville house. She succeeded well enough that she could even afford to dress the girls fashionably—in identical outfits as the custom of the day dictated.

Caroline Hardee Godfrey, for whom I was named, could have easily provided for both girls; she owned a peach plantation and a fine ante-bellum house staffed with servants. A capable and energetic woman who had married into a prominent family, Caroline restored the house and its gardens, wrote poetry, and published a book of spiritual essays. My mother never forgot that as Caroline's adopted daughter she could have had a finishing school education, come out into society as a debutante,

Louise and May at two years old, 1911
(twins holding each other's hands)

worn beautiful clothes, and traveled, to New York, Paris, and wherever fine young ladies were taken. Her visits to Atlanta only made her life in Louisville less acceptable.

The twins, beautiful as babies, grew up to be beautiful women, and local photographers missed no opportunity to record their two-fold charm. My father Russell Teague was a medical student at the University of Louisville, and he became smitten by Louise, whom he met when he rented a room at Lulie's boarding house.

Louise and May, 1920

They married in 1929, the year he finished his internship (she was 20 and he was 24) and they immediately headed for eastern Kentucky where he set up a practice in family medicine.

Pikeville, in the heartland of the Appalachians, was not to my mother's liking then, and it would not be so now. Today, you might go there to hike one of the Hatfield-McCoy River Trails or to paddle a kayak on the Big Sandy River. Or you might admire the site where Mayor William Hambley spent 14 years and almost $80 million moving a mountain—at least a part of it—to reroute the railroad tracks because the coal-hauling trains spewed pollutants as they rumbled through town. Life in Pikeville in no way resembled the elegant existence of Aunt Caroline Godfrey to which Louise aspired.

My dad, however, had grown up in rural Kentucky in the small mining town of Providence, where his father owned a store. My dad had inherited the down-to-earth quality of his own mother, a woman who started Sunday dinner by wringing a chicken's neck, and then after cleaning and plucking the bird, made biscuits and gravy and a pie or two to go along with it. Pikeville, its lifestyle, and its inhabitants were comfortable and familiar to my father.

Mother, on the other hand, disdained the "hill people," the hillbillies, who seemed foreign and primitive to her. If dad was called to deliver a baby "over yonder," she sometimes had to join him on horseback to go over the next hill to administer chloroform during the delivery.

Louise, 1923

Russell and Louise, 1929

Dad later jokingly described these scenes: my mother feeling faint as she held the chloroform over the laboring woman's face; the husband and a couple of other men leaning against the walls watching. During his efforts, dad was privately worrying that, if something went wrong with the birth, the men might be tempted to use the shotguns they had brought along for the event. Because the Depression began just as dad opened his practice, he was frequently paid with eggs or "undressed" chickens, which mother had to clean and pluck, another reason to dislike Pikeville. With mother's support and, most likely at her insistence, dad applied to graduate school at Johns Hopkins University in Baltimore. Equipped with a degree in public health, he returned to Pikeville to take charge of training midwives, which put an end to the horseback trips over the mountains and provided a steady income.

Russell with the midwives in Pikeville, Kentucky, 1931

My brother Russell Jr., nicknamed Rusty, was born in 1932, and I arrived in 1935. Rusty, like my mother, was a beautiful baby, as she frequently pointed out to me, but my looks disappointed her, since I was not the adorable girl baby she had wanted. That year we left Pikeville for Paducah, where my father became city health officer, a step up the ladder, which pleased my mother. We moved to the Charleston Apartments in a fine residential neighborhood on Jefferson Street.

In 1937, the Ohio River rose above its 50-foot flood level, inundating Paducah and driving us and some 27,000 other people from our homes. The rising water forced us from our ground floor apartment up to the second floor and then to the third floor, where we huddled until a boat arrived to evacuate us. My mother, brother, and I boarded the train to Atlanta where Aunt Caroline Godfrey took us in, while dad remained in Paducah dealing with public health problems. Most of our belongings were lost when the apartment was flooded, and we arrived in Georgia with only the clothes on our backs. Our arrival as bedraggled refugees humiliated my mother, concerned as she was about appearances.

Mother had thought that by marrying a doctor she would enjoy the prestige of her husband's position and have enough money to make up for the life she might have had as Caroline Godfrey's daughter on the peach plantation. She had anticipated romantic candlelight dinners with "Smoke Gets In Your Eyes," their song, playing softly in the background. But two small children put an end to

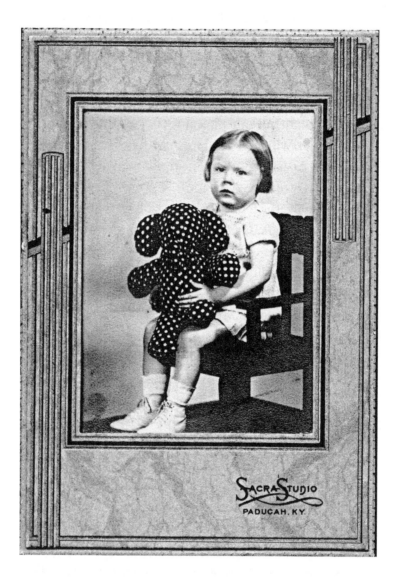

Caroline, 1937

candlelight dinners, and mother became more and more disillusioned. She had expected something better out of marriage than the drudgeries and hardships of everyday existence, which were worsened by the Depression.

My brother and I were too young to remember the Depression, but we were told and retold the stories of unemployed men lining up in front of soup kitchens, men in overcoats and fedoras, as well as those in jackets and caps. We heard again and again how the Wall Street crash had cost Herbert Hoover his presidency and how Franklin Roosevelt saved the country from ruin with his New Deal programs. Dad considered himself extremely fortunate to have a job with the city of Paducah.

My parents moved up in the world again when the state health department in Louisville offered my dad a job. My mother's newfound sense of well-being, however, was marred one evening as they were returning home from Aunt May's. A drunk driver swerved out from a roadhouse and crashed into the passenger side of their car. Dad escaped with a few cracked ribs, but mother, who took the brunt of the impact, sustained leg injuries and a cut over her left eye that required surgery. Although she recovered physically she continued to suffer psychologically because her face, the source of much of her self-satisfaction, was permanently scarred; the fact that May remained undamaged made the injury worse.

Aunt May and my mother shared not only their physical appearances but also a psychic bond (or so they thought): when Aunt May heard the ambulance racing to the accident, she knew intuitively that her twin had been injured. Less pleasantly, both suffered personality changes when they drank too much. May's husband, Oscar Kunkel, banned alcohol at home early in their marriage but dad either would not or could not do the same. When I was seven, sick with the measles and not permitted out of my darkened bedroom, I heard mother and May downstairs, their voices raised. The argument ended with the crash of breaking glass, a mirror as it turned out, as another night of drinking deteriorated into a "sisterly fight." I lay in my bed shaking, and sometimes even now relive the fear that I felt that night listening to their violent anger.

My adoptive grandmother Lulie also disapproved of drinking, so when she was at our house my parents sneaked drinks in the pantry rather than openly enjoying cocktails. They didn't stop after a drink or two, but continued until they had emptied the bottle of bourbon, their chosen form of alcohol. Prohibition, which went into effect in 1920, may have played a part in mother's drinking problem by making hard liquor more convenient than beer or wine. Because the Volstead Act prohibited the production and sale of alcohol, but not its consumption, people carried their flasks into restaurants and poured their contraband liquor into their soft drinks.

When I was too young to know what was causing my mother's strange behavior, I thought that I had a "double mother," and I did not mean her twin sister. One "mother" was pretty, kind, and warm; she sang and played the piano; she smelled like flowers and honey and kissed me good night every evening. She was my own personal Fairy Godmother. But without warning Wicked Mother would appear, one eyebrow raised, her face distorted. She slurred, spoke hurtful words, and smelled "icky," as I described to myself the alcoholic sweetness. When I grew older, I realized that it was alcohol that transformed my Fairy Godmother into the Wicked Mother, just as I realized that my mother's drinking problem escalated in tandem with her unhappiness.

As I began to see patterns in her behavior, I learned to stay out of the line of fire. The drinking usually started in the early evening while mother was fixing dinner and

Rusty, Louise, and Caroline, 1939

continued until my parents went to bed. Sometimes I went outside into the yard behind the kitchen to check her through the window, watching carefully for warning signs like the raised right eyebrow. If I caught her hovering close to the kitchen cabinet where she sometimes stashed a bottle and snitching a drink, I knew that this was going to be "one of those nights." I tried to become small and quiet, not to upset her. Dad also drank, but the bourbon did not affect him the way it did my mother. As an adult I understand how liquor can change a personality or exaggerate certain traits, but as a child I could not fathom alcohol's transformative power.

One night when mother had been drinking, a loud noise downstairs near the kitchen woke me up. The next day when she appeared bruised and battered, I figured out that she had fallen down the basement stairs, but no one mentioned the cuts and bandages on her body and face, and she herself acted as if nothing had happened. I worried that she could be badly hurt, even killed, and that I would never know what had happened to her since no one would talk about it.

⌣

Quite early I was taught or figured out that some subjects should never be mentioned, even within the family. My mother believed that contentious conversations disturbed digestion, so she laid down rules about what could and could not be discussed at the table. Because we were forbidden to talk about politics, money, or religion, and because we were seldom together except at meal times, we never discussed these things at all. Other taboos included death, sex, biological functions, and certain relatives who had fallen out of favor. But of all the taboos, the most powerful was the secret, which we never discussed among ourselves and certainly never revealed to the rest of the world: my mother's drinking problem.

After mother fell down the stairs, the basement began to obsess me. It was a dark, mysterious place where my father and brother exercised their creative powers, but where I was forbidden to go. When Rusty was making toy soldiers, melting lead and pouring it into molds, I would stand at the top of the stairs tantalized by the smell of the molten lead, but couldn't get close enough to watch him. Dad had a darkroom in the basement where he turned film into photographs, but I couldn't watch that either, even though (or maybe especially because) the process appeared to be magic. I was also curious about the "stoker" that relieved dad of the backbreaking job of shoveling coal, but that too was off limits. The basement, fascinating as it was, remained the exclusive territory of the males in our family.

If being forbidden to go into the basement made me feel the unfairness of being a girl, the requirement to be a "good girl," was even more upsetting. "Be nice, be good, don't get angry. Share your candy, share your ice cream and your toys, be sweet, be sweet Caroline, Sweet Ca-ro-line." I heard that refrain all through my childhood, with the requirements getting tougher as I grew older; to the orders to be sweet and kind were added "don't pout, don't complain, be a nice girl, be a good girl, be helpful." Later as I approached adulthood, I was admonished for any infraction of perfect sweetness. If I ever sighed at the unfairness of something, my mother spelled out "E-R-R-O-R" in a loud voice. All this conditioning created a submissive child, if not a completely selfless one. I had learned my lesson well, though I always felt that there was a stronger part of me that lay dormant. My awareness of that part of me and what I could do with it came later in my life, but it was nurtured by my adoptive grandmother, Lulie, who came to live with us in Louisville when I was still small.

⌣

Lulie was then in her 60s, a petite Victorian lady. She dressed conservatively and piled her thinning hair high on her head, folding it back and forth to make it look thicker. Aside from the comb that held her hair in place, her only adornment was a brooch pinned at her collar, with the profile bust of a young woman carved out of white shell and set onto an oval of polished black onyx. I inherited the brooch, which still brings up the image of Lulie, sitting on the rose brocade love seat in our living room, her ankles politely crossed, our dog Gabby snuggling up to her as she read the newspaper or mended my father's socks with a wooden darning egg. Age had reduced her to a frail, nervous, birdlike figure, her skin transparent, her hands boney.

But I was happy when I was with Lulie, for she gave me special gifts, her love and trust, when I most needed them. I'm not sure I knew what love was all about, but I remember how it felt. I knew that I could rely on her to be the same gentle, kind woman I loved in return; she would never change into someone else as my mother did; she was always Lulie, her face shining with tenderness and approval. Lulie kept a diary in 1942 and almost every day she wrote something to the effect that "my Caroline fills

Lulie with Gabby, Louisville, 1941

my life with joy." I clearly remember how she looked when I came into her room. She would throw her hands up with delight; her face was bright with pleasure and her smile

Tintype of Lulie, age 12, when she visited her mother in 1882

was pure sunshine. On summer afternoons when I was three or four, she would give me a bath, dust me with baby powder, and we would take our afternoon naps together, lulled to sleep by the breeze and the whir of the rotating electric fan. Even now, a whiff of baby powder reawakens the quiet security I felt with her. I truly believe that my confidence in her love later gave me the courage to step outside my prescribed role as "good girl" and find qualities that I only gradually recognized that I possessed.

Lulie's life, the little that I know about it, had its own secrets. In 1942 she wrote in her diary of falling ill and believing she would die, but she didn't tell us about it; she didn't even name the disease, either fearing it might be "catching" or else because it affected a body part that Victorian ladies simply did not mention. Lulie never spoke of being sent as a nine-year-old to live with her uncle when her parents divorced or of her father's subsequent marriage to a first cousin. She never mentioned his life in Florida with his new wife and their daughter, whom Lulie always referred to as her cousin, but who was in reality her half-sister; she never mentioned her separation from her brother and sister who were sent Out West to work on a farm. Later she refused to acknowledge that she had a brother. Why had her parents divorced? Why were she and her siblings not able to stay with their mother? What had happened to the brother whose existence she could not acknowledge? I never found out.

⁓

World War II hovered in the background of my childhood, not a secret like mother's drinking, but something the adults spoke about quietly or behind closed doors, presumably to keep from frightening Rusty and me. Of course, as a youngster of seven, I did not understand or even want to understand what the adults were talking about. We were taught what to do during practice air raids both at home and at school, but I was not sure why it helped for us to sit on the floor and be silent as imaginary bombs dropped around us.

I could sense that Lulie was anxious about the war. Her fingers sometimes twitched nervously, tapping out a song on an invisible piano, and when I asked why Lulie drummed her fingers, mother answered that Lulie was afraid of the dark. In fact, Lulie was probably afraid of the possibilities opened up by the war, afraid that my father would be drafted. When she listened to the news on the radio, she would murmur "Oh dear, oh dear," and when things sounded really grim, she would blurt out, "Dog take it!," which was as close as she ever got to swearing, something Victorian ladies did not do. Once a week, her sister Clara May, my real grandmother, would come over to hear President Roosevelt's "fireside chat." I didn't understand what the president was saying, but I could tell that it upset the two ladies; even though he spoke reassuringly and despite the immense confidence they had in him, he could not put their fears to rest.

For the war effort we made tin-foil balls from chewing gum wrappers, bought war bonds with money we had saved or been given, and we became aware of the rationing of shoes, gasoline, rubber tires, and sugar. We took great pride in dad's victory garden and ate tomatoes, spinach, peas, and even okra because our patriotic duty required it. Cartoonish propaganda posters convinced us to hate Nazis and "Japs." With the neighborhood children Rusty and I played "hospital" and "war," which blended elements of cowboys and Indians, cops and robbers with spies and counterspies who had secret codes and passwords not to be shared with adults. In "war" the boys fought the battles, while we girls cleaned up and bandaged the wounded. It did not occur to us that our father might be called up to go to the actual war.

On summer evenings, we played tag, hide-and-go-seek, and kick the can. On rainy days we played "doctor," second in popularity after "war" because we got to see the secret places of each other's bodies. As far as I could tell, the boys' "wienies" were the only things that made them boys and not girls, warriors and not nurses. My friends and I knew not to tell our parents about the "doctor" game, which became one of the first secrets we had of our own.

On Saturday mornings as I helped my mother dust the living room furniture, we listened to "Let's Pretend," a radio program sponsored by Cream of Wheat. The show featured classic fairy stories with their standard glass slippers, golden rings, and magic carpets. All the episodes ended happily: ogres were defeated and wicked stepmothers became fairy godmothers. Pretending was a big part of my life, something private that belonged to me alone. Sometimes it was difficult to know what was real and what was pretend, especially in terms of religion. My grandmother listened to my prayers every night and told me that to have them answered, I would have to be a good girl. Because my prayers went unanswered, I thought that praying might be the same as pretending. Or, maybe God didn't answer my prayers because of the "doctor" game.

The war ended and my father took a position with the Phipps Institute in Philadelphia, an organization devoted to tuberculosis research and associated with the University of Pennsylvania. We moved to Wayne, part of the Main Line, a collection of wealthy suburbs accessible from Philly by commuter train. My dad became health commissioner of Pennsylvania in 1950, another welcome step up socially and financially. Though his job moved to Harrisburg, we continued to live in Wayne, so that I could finish high school there, and it didn't hurt my mother's social aspirations that my dad was chauffeured to and from his job in a state-owned Cadillac.

I attended Radnor High School, where I got my first inkling of my "real" self, the person I might become, someone beyond the "good girl" my mother was training me to be. I participated in theater groups, became captain of several sports teams, and discovered that I had leadership qualities. I enjoyed my friends, but did not invite them to my house or ask a guy in after a date for fear that mother might be passed out on the dining room floor, something that happened more than once.

I graduated in 1952 and left home for Goucher College in Baltimore, where after some false starts I decided that I would major in art history. The Post-Impressionists especially attracted me, not only for their color choices and the freedom of their style, but for their freedom to follow their artistic and personal desires. Nevertheless my past followed me in the form of late night phone calls from the Wicked Mother. I had a wonderful roommate, but couldn't fully confide in her, because I had to hide the shame of my mother's drinking problem. It would be many years before I could say out loud to someone that my mother was an alcoholic. I can remember the day when I finally said it and the feeling that a heavy weight had lifted and that I had gained a new lightness of mind and spirit. By then, however, I had been dealt another secret, one perhaps more dark and damaging than the Wicked Mother.

Knox, about two years old, c. 1935

CHAPTER 4
KNOX: BROWNWOOD TO LOUISVILLE

My husband Knox spent his early years moving from place to place in the wake of his father's academic career. He was born in Chicago, moved to Cambridge, and then Nashville; when he was nine, he spent two months in the Maryland countryside while his father worked for the OSS. In the immediate aftermath of his father's death Knox and his little brother stayed briefly in Pennsylvania with the family of an OSS colleague, and then he found himself back in Texas, where the Chandler family had its roots.

As an only child until he was six, Knox, then called Pachy, enjoyed his parents' undivided attention. Encouraged to be outgoing and bold, he enjoyed making people laugh. When he was two, his parents took a sabbatical in Europe and he stayed in Texas with Aunt Bettie, who gallantly offered to take him for five months. Bettie recognized Knox's childhood facility for humor, and she recorded his antics in a journal so that his parents would not miss his pranks and bright sayings. He ran away, but explained he could cross a busy street because "man took my hand." He peed on the back yard dirt pile, justifying his naughtiness by saying, "I making mud." When a visitor put several spoonfuls of sugar into his teacup, Pachy admonished in a mash-up of English and Spanish, "too mas, too mas." Everyone laughed, which pleased him, so when the visitor began pouring milk into the cup, Pachy repeated "too mas, too mas" and looked around hopefully for the reaction.

It cannot have been easy for the boys to lose their father and then be separated from their mother. In the chaotic period after the tragedy, Colston was sent to live with relatives, first in Batesville, Arkansas, and later in San Antonio. When he was ten, Knox stayed for a year with his Great Aunt Elizabeth, known as Libbut, the divorced sister of Margaret's mother, who was close enough to Margaret that she had stitched up her college wardrobe and trousseau. Libbut had retired as a social worker and in 1944 was running a lunch counter in tiny Tuleta, Texas, whose population even now is only 292 people. Knox remembers no more than snatches of his life in Tuleta, for example that Aunt Libbut, who told him that "distance made his guitar playing sound better," sent him off to play under "yonder live oak tree." There was no "foolin' around" with Libbut, who rose to the challenge of caring for a pre-adolescent boy and saw that he kept to the straight and narrow.

Meanwhile Margaret, perhaps influenced by Aunt Libbut's choice of career, completed her degree in social work. She and the boys moved to San Antonio to live near her sisters and her sister-in-law Bettie, where Knox enjoyed antagonizing his teenage girl cousins by listening to country music on the radio at top volume. He offered to play his guitar for anyone who would listen, accompanying himself as he sang mournful cowboy songs. He even persuaded the local radio station to let him perform on

the air early in the morning so that his mother could hear him before she went to work. She turned on the radio to be greeted with Knox's rendition of "Mommy Won't You Please Stay Home With Me?," a performance on which she never commented.

After two years in San Antonio, Margaret took a job as a child welfare worker in Brownwood and moved in with her mother-in-law, Carrie Chandler. She insisted on paying rent for her half of the house, something about which she always remained proud. Because Carrie's husband, S. E. Chandler, had died in 1944, a year after W. K.'s death, the presence of Margaret and the boys must have comforted the widow.

Knox and Colston grew up in Brownwood, going to local schools and the Presbyterian Church, which they were required to attend twice on Sunday. The rest of the week they lived with the restrictions S. E. had imposed on their father: no swearing, drinking, smoking, or playing cards. They were, however, allowed to dance with girls, though when teens gathered in the high school gymnasium for parties, chaperones pulled out rulers and measured the distance between the boys and girls, to make sure the couples kept a virtuous distance apart.

Bashful and awkward like many teenagers, Knox enjoyed playing practical jokes, especially when he could carry off a good one without getting caught. When he hid burning sulfur under a classroom radiator, the teachers could not find the source of the rotten egg smell any more than they could discover who was responsible. He had friends, he dated girls and he played the trombone, becoming captain of the marching band, a job he took seriously despite his reputation as a jokester.

Each year Grandfather Colston took him on a three-day dove-hunting trip to a family ranch near Breckenridge, Texas, where he learned to shoot a 12-gauge shotgun. As he tells it, the first day out, he would miss all the birds; the second day out he would miss every other one, but by the third day he got them all. His mother never joined them; she always had work to do.

Knox excelled in school, especially in math. At his high school graduation he gave the valedictory address, not because he was first in his class, but because the two students who outranked him were girls and therefore ineligible, something that says a lot about attitudes in Brownwood in 1949.

⌣

Knox found his way into science only after several false starts. When he graduated from high school, not yet seventeen, he had no idea what he wanted to do with his life. He enrolled at Washington and Lee University (W & L), because Mrs. Jessie Ball DuPont, a close friend of Aunt Helen Knox and a philanthropic supporter of W & L, had agreed to pay for his education there. Knox thought that science might appeal to him, though he had not taken the Brownwood High School's one science course, biology. When he discovered that W & L didn't have the math and physics offerings he wanted, he applied to Johns Hopkins University, which awarded him a full-tuition graduate scholarship, even before he had completed his undergraduate work. The scholarship did not pay for living expenses, and Jessie DuPont, though aware of his financial need, refused to pay for his further education unless he first completed a liberal arts degree at W & L. Knox turned down the Hopkins scholarship and after the first semester of his junior year went home for the Christmas break and never returned to W & L.

After a stint at the University of Texas where the large class size put him off, he hitchhiked to Louisville, Kentucky, thinking he might enlist as a pilot in the Air Force. Relatives on the Colston side of the family, the Embrys, took Knox under their wing, taught him to drink bourbon and branch water, and advised him to go to medical school. He finished his undergraduate degree and enrolled in the University of Louisville medical school, class of 1959, but realized quickly that he was not cut out to be a clinician, even though his Aunt Janet Embry thought he had "a good bedside manner." Nor did the medical school curriculum include the kind of science that intrigued him.

Knox discovered his calling in the basement of the medical school building, where Dr. Warren Rehm was using electrical methods to study acid secretion in the stomach. It was innovative work that contributed to the evolution of research in the 1960s, as the study of physiology refocused on cells and their machinery rather than organ systems. Knox found in Dr. Rehm a mentor who understood him and appreciated his intellectual abilities (as well as his sense of humor). Rehm invited Knox to join his scientific team and attend national physiology and biophysics meetings. Knox found the experience wonderful and challenging and although he did graduate with an MD degree, not a PhD, his work with Dr. Rehm propelled him into a career of scientific research.

CHAPTER 5
CAROLINE: GOUCHER TO LOUISVILLE

While Knox was finding his life's direction in Dr. Rehm's lab, I was finishing my studies at Goucher College. I had majored in art history and lined up a job at the Fogg Museum in Boston. I was twenty-one, yearning to work in the art world, and looking forward to living on my own for the first time. Boston, a cultural Mecca, beckoned to me.

My parents came to Baltimore to enjoy my graduation, but the night before the ceremony mother was hospitalized for emergency abdominal surgery. As class president, I had responsibilities at the graduation, but managed to get to the hospital for an hour. Mother was hooked up to various bags and machines, and despite our differences I felt sad seeing her so sick and vulnerable. She recovered slowly and only after a month in the hospital was able to travel home to Kentucky, still needing nursing care. Although I didn't realize it, mother's illness changed my future.

In 1955 my father had returned to Louisville as Kentucky state health commissioner, a position he would hold for 16 years under four governors. The job was prestigious but demanding, requiring travel to meetings all over Kentucky and beyond. I understood without having to be told that dad would not have considered letting a stranger into the apartment to take care of mother, so I put my dreams of Boston on hold and took over, looking after her and preparing our meals, despite my lack of experience in the kitchen. Since mother had a low opinion of my culinary skills, we were fortunate that the Mayflower Apartments had a dining room. When a second surgery set back mother's recovery, I stayed on, willing to do anything to help dad, who, in return, offered to take over the nursing duties after dinner so that I could have a social life.

I had endured four years of blind dates at a women's college and was not enthusiastic about another one, so when a childhood friend, Neville Caudill, suggested that I go out with his medical school classmate, I was reluctant. I was dating several men and had no desire to meet someone new. But my dad thought I should not turn down Neville's offer, since he and Neville's father, Fred Caudill, had been colleagues and, after Fred had died of bulbar polio, dad had helped the Caudill family get back on its feet.

So I dutifully told Neville that yes, I would be happy to meet his friend. Neville described his classmate as polite and very bright, adding that his attractive qualities included a Texas drawl and the ability to play the guitar, which appealed to me. I even liked his name, Knox Chandler. The only hitch regarding the date was that Knox was doing research on stomach ulcers and the in vivo dog experiments continued as long as the dog lived, sometimes for hours and hours.[1] Neville explained that Knox would be free to go out on Saturday night "if the dog died." After I accepted the date, Knox's first three experiments lasted late into the night; only when the dog died shortly into the fourth experiment did I have the opportunity to meet Knox Chandler.

Knox turned out to be good looking, friendly and courteous in the traditional Southern way, with a twinkle in his eyes that made him seem as if we had met before. When he kissed me goodnight on that first date, I felt that the relationship was very right and went to bed wondering if he felt the same way. He always claimed that he only kissed me on the forehead, but I can still recall the sensation on my lips as if the kiss happened yesterday. The more we saw of one another, the more we felt that we had been fated to meet.

Late in the fall after returning from the national physiology meetings in Rochester, Knox phoned to take me to a party given by his aunt. The evening turned out bright and clear, the air scented with autumn leaves, and as we drove through Cherokee Park, Knox pulled over and rolled down the window. Everything seemed perfect, except the look on his face. I thought he might be coming down with something or was going to be sick, and I didn't know what to do. Gradually it became clear that Knox wanted to tell me something, but didn't know how to begin. After a few starts, he said he had had lunch

---

1 The idea of working on live dogs did not bother me then, though it does now.

in Rochester with Joan Thayer, my college roommate, and had surprised himself by pouring out his feelings about me. Knox paused and had trouble getting started again.

"When I learned that you had dated other men while I was gone, I realized that I was jealous, terribly jealous. I knew that I wanted to marry you."

His expression of love swept me away. As he put his arm around me, I caught my breath and stuttered out my answer.

"I missed you so much. The dates, the others, mean nothing to me. I feel the same way about you."

I think we were both surprised that the blind date had turned so quickly into the desire to get married. I'm not positive, but I think Knox asked, "Will you marry me?"

Maybe he didn't, but I answered without hesitating for a second, "Yes, oh, yes, I want to be your wife, more than anything."

I was thrilled that this wonderful man wanted me. As always when I am uncontrollably happy, I started to cry. Tears rolled down my cheeks as we kissed and then laughed the blissful laugh of two people who feel happily connected. We had known each other only a couple of months. I was 21 and Knox 22. Although I was unsure whether we were experienced enough to know what we wanted in our life partners, I did not for one moment think about my commitment to go to Boston or my need to strike out on my own.

The next day as we talked about my meeting his mother, he pulled a picture from his wallet, the image of a middle-aged woman with an air of authority. What surprised me was the format of the photo, a workplace ID, not something more personal; still the fact that Knox carried it in his wallet suggested he and his mother had a close relationship.

Handing it to me Knox remarked, "It's sad that she doesn't have much fun anymore." Or maybe he said, "It's sad, she isn't much fun anymore." I didn't want to ask and he didn't volunteer more, except to say that his brother Colston, six years younger, was still in high school. Since Knox had not mentioned his father, I hesitated about mentioning him. Maybe his parents were divorced. But curiosity led me on.

"He is dead, he committed suicide during World War II," came the unexpected answer to my cautious question. I tried to hide my shock.

"I'm so sorry," I said automatically. "How terrible, how tragic! Was he in the army?"

"No, in the OSS. I was just a boy. I don't remember much about it." He said this almost without emotion, as if he were describing what he had eaten for breakfast or the weather.

"He was the head instructor at the OSS training school, in charge of training spies before they went overseas," he added in a way that shut down the conversation.

I found it sad that Knox had so few memories of the father who had abandoned him, especially since I had warm memories of my own father, many from around the time I was ten. But Knox didn't seem to want to continue with the subject, so we turned to his plans for his future. Dr. Rehm had suggested that after graduation he join the Public Health Service at the National Institutes of Health in Maryland and work with the eminent biophysicist Kenneth S. Cole. It would be a two-year stint which had the bonus of satisfying his requirement for military service.

A few days later Knox formally asked my father for my hand in marriage, explaining his plan to switch from clinical medicine to research. The interview went well. Dad gave us his blessing and mother seemed happy, though she turned to me and said, "You know, 'if the dog dies' will be the story of your married life." We all laughed, but her prediction would turn out to be accurate.

I loved Knox and respected him for all his good traits. With traditional Southern courtesy he opened doors for me, pulled out my chair, and lit my cigarettes. (Yes, we both smoked back then.) He had a good sense of humor and told jokes with perfect timing. When I found out that he kept a crib sheet of punch lines in his pocket, I still admired his style and the fact that he laughed a lot, even at himself.

I was struck by his intelligence, as were his friends and relatives. Dr. Rehm, who appreciated Knox for his quick wit as well as his intellect, pulled me aside to tell me that Knox had a great career ahead of him in science. Dr. Rehm's words also implied that as his wife I should support that career.

Although Knox and I were strongly attracted physically and spent time getting to know each other's bodies and emotions, wanting to go "all the way" (as we called it in the 1950s), we decided to keep sex for marriage and remained virgins until our wedding night. Today many people, including ourselves, consider that attitude "old school," but we were products of our puritanical upbringing, especially Knox.

From the beginning, everything about our relationship seemed right to me, as if I had found the other half of myself. What I wanted more than anything was to have a good marriage and to raise a family in a happy and open environment, but I also swore to myself that I would not stand in the way of Knox's career. Today I can see how these two desires conflicted, but back then there was no way of knowing what lay ahead. We were in love and certain that we could handle anything.

Mother's alcoholism continued to plague me. Dad continued to pretend that it did not exist and for several months after her operation they had no alcohol in the apartment. But that did not last. For the next three years in Louisville, I was afraid her drinking problem would resurface, most likely in a nasty and embarrassing way, and I would have to address the subject with Knox. Though I did not want to take my family secret into my marriage, I was doing just that.

PART 2

There are no secrets that time does not reveal.

Jean Racine, *Britannicus* (1669)

After the wedding, June 1957

CHAPTER 6
MARRIAGE AND MOTHERHOOD

Over the Christmas holidays in 1956 we drove to Texas with my parents to meet Knox's mother. Although he assured me that everything would be fine, that his mother would love me, I felt nervous. Margaret greeted us warmly and showed us around her apartment, which had an air of impermanence, with unpacked boxes from her recent move stacked against the walls. She was reserved, but her manner was pleasant and as the conversation flowed easily, I began to relax.

I noticed that she smiled adoringly at Knox, but that the smile faded when he left the room and she found herself alone with me. Late in the afternoon we were in the kitchen where she was fixing artichokes for dinner. Because the only artichokes I had ever eaten were in a salad and had come straight from a can, I was watching closely to see how she planned to cook the exotic vegetables.

Suddenly her demeanor changed. She reset her shoulders, crossed her arms, and squared off facing me, like a mother bear protecting her cub.

"Why do you want to marry my son?" she demanded to know.

I was caught off guard. The hostility of her question reduced me to a timid, voiceless blockhead. I wanted to flee, but was rooted in place. Couldn't she see that Knox and I loved each other? Knox's folks back in Louisville could see our compatibility and our pleasure in one another's company; they didn't need to be told the reasons. With hindsight I can think of many answers. I could have said I wanted to marry him for his kind and tender manner, or because we felt complete together, or because I was certain that our trust and love would only grow with time. If she had presented her question affectionately or humorously or had put me at ease in some small way, I might have been able to tell her how deeply I loved her son. I have no idea what I actually did say, probably something stupid, trite, or flippant, something like "he is so witty, so smart and, uh, plays the guitar." I'm pretty sure I didn't mention his sex appeal, but maybe I didn't say anything at all, for Knox came back into the kitchen, rescuing me from the need to defend myself. Margaret's face lit up as before, her hostility melted away, and she acted as if she had never threatened me, as if we had been chatting pleasantly all the time. I was shaken, and it was not until years later that I learned what she had been thinking that day in the kitchen.

The next day, Margaret drove us to San Antonio where we met members of the Chandler and Knox clans for lunch. At the time we didn't notice that no one represented the Colston side of the family, even though Margaret's two sisters lived right in San Antonio. Years later I discovered that Margaret had not been on good terms with the female members of her family for a long time. The Knox family, however, was well represented: Grandmother Carrie, her missionary brother Rob and his wife, and her unmarried sister Helen. Carrie's father, William Alexander Knox, a business man and founder of the first bank in Giddings, Texas, had made certain that all six of his children, three boys and three girls, received college educations at the University of Texas.

Helen Knox, the youngest, graduated in 1908, earning not only her diploma but also an athletic letter in tennis. Helen became a banker in New York, and played an important role in my husband's life, getting him started with a university education, entertaining him in New York during Christmas break of his freshman year at Washington and Lee, and helping Margaret Chandler after her husband's death.

I was also introduced to Knox's brother Colston, who was 16, pleasant but shy. I enjoyed meeting the Knoxes and Chandlers at the lunch party, but I couldn't forget the incident with Margaret in the kitchen. Still I was thankful for the way she had raised her sons, especially the man I was to marry.

—

Despite her earlier antagonism, Knox's mother appeared to accept our engagement and planned to come to Louisville for the wedding in June, arranging with her father's sister, her aunt Janet Embry, for the rehearsal dinner at the Louisville Country Club where the Embrys belonged.

My own mother had her way concerning the wedding arrangements, though she left to me the actual writing of the invitations and other tasks. Most of the wedding gifts we received reflected her taste, which ran to the floral and the formal. Her home always blossomed with flowered rugs, flowered curtains, flowered chintz slipcovers, even flowered wallpaper. My own preferences were simpler, and I would have chosen pottery and stainless steel, but she virtually ordered me to pick out traditional patterns for china, crystal and silver because "if I didn't get them for my wedding, I never would have them." She, like most of the invited wedding guests, expected that Knox would become a physician; we would entertain like other successful Louisville doctors, and the servants would shine the silver. I could not go against her tastes in china and silver any more than I could reject her other wishes or break the taboos that surrounded her alcoholism.

Looking back, I wonder if Knox's choice of research and my encouragement were also choices in life style. Neither of us wanted a large medical practice with all its social and financial implications. As it turned out, we dragged around the silver flatware, serving dishes, pitchers, coffee and tea sets, platters, butter dishes, and ice buckets for fifty years, while I used pottery and stainless steel. Maybe we hung on to the silver and crystal because we were sentimentally attached to the people who had chosen the gifts, but I now think we kept them because they were part of the unacknowledged baggage of our Southern upbringing.

Dr. William Benfield, pastor of the Highland Presbyterian Church, conducted our pre-nuptial counseling. We met together, separately, and again together, something unusual for the 1950s. When I wasn't present Dr. Benfield asked Knox what he didn't like about me. Knox replied that he didn't like the way I played bridge; I talked about other things instead of concentrating. When asked the same question about Knox, I answered that I didn't like the way he played bridge; he took the game too seriously. Although the counseling was not otherwise helpful, we wisely never again played bridge together. We realized that we would be wrong to try to change one another, especially concerning traits so deeply rooted in our personalities, my feeling that a game was a form of communication and a way to have fun, and Knox's opinion that games are like wars, contests you did your utter best to win.

After the final session, Dr. Benfield presented us with a thin booklet, "Sex in Marriage," which contained about eight poorly drawn positions for the newly married couple—a puritanical version of the Kama Sutra! Dr. Benfield performed the marriage ceremony June 8, 1957. The wedding and reception went without a hitch, although Knox, weak in the knees, wondered for a moment what he was getting into. As we left the church, the photographer snapped us standing in front of the sign announcing next Sunday's sermon, whose topic was the Last Judgment.

We decided on a week's honeymoon in a log cabin in Brown County State Park. Because Knox insisted on paying, the price was right; because he had to take medical boards at the end of that week, the distance was ideal, 90 miles from Louisville. I do not recommend waiting until your wedding night to have intercourse. It is not the right time to experience that intimacy for the first time, but Knox was a considerate and tender lover. We laughed at our awkwardness and agreed that we would have a lifetime together—to practice. Although Knox had brought a trunk full of books to study, he didn't crack one of them. It was a wonderful honeymoon.

We were young and inexperienced in many ways. Although I had given up my chance to go to Boston to follow my interest in art, I did so knowing that I was choosing to marry a man who, like me, felt that we were fortunate to have found each other. What we had going for us was sheer youthful excitement, love, and interest in sharing a life—whatever it turned out to be.

⌣

Our first two years of marriage coincided with Knox's last two of medical school. We rented a four-room apartment in a building owned by an organization that assisted people who had suffered mental and emotional breakdowns. Our apartment was spacious, comfortable, and affordable at $65 a month, furnished in what we called "Early Marriage," mostly borrowed pieces from relatives. Anything more elegant wouldn't have made us happier.

One night, shortly after we had moved into our apartment, Knox was getting ready to attend a bachelor party. When I asked what time he would be home, he responded as if I had asked a stupid question, that he had no idea when the party would end, that in fact it might go on all night. With the virtue of hindsight, I know I was worrying about being alone in the old house with the only available telephone downstairs where the clients of Recovery Incorporated. met. His answer reminded me of the conditions that kept postponing our first date, only this time it was "if the dog dies, I'll be home." His life and activities mattered; mine were secondary. Was this to be the story of my life as my mother had predicted? Was this his nature, and would I just have to adjust to it?

I had taken a job as Dr. Rehm's secretary, in the basement laboratory across the hall from the morgue. It was a good job with a friendly group of scientists, but after I became pregnant in October, the fumes from the morgue made me queasy. When the job ended the following June, a month before the baby was due, our already strict budget got even tighter. For the remaining ten months of Knox's medical school career we lived on my savings of $2,000; our monthly budget of $200 allotted $65 for rent, $65 for food, and $70 for everything else. The baby was born July 20th, a healthy eight-pound boy whom we named William Knox Chandler after his father and grandfather.

All in all, our first years together went very well, despite the many adjustments. Knox focused on becoming a scientist while fulfilling his medical school requirements. He was often preoccupied, so that the little courtesies of courtship—lighting my cigarette, pulling out my chair, opening the door for me—became a thing of the past. While he worked at his career, I devoted myself to acquiring secretarial skills, keeping house, managing laundry, and learning to cook, at which I was a beginner. My mother wasn't much help in this. She had learned by watching the cooks at Lulie's boarding house, and if I wanted to try one of her specialties, I would have to watch her and write down what she did as she added a handful of this or two of that. Margaret's letters included index cards with recipes, which turned out to be helpful. Many involved opening cans and combining their contents: opening a can of cream of mushroom soup, adding a can of peas plus one of sausages, mixing well, heating, then pouring the whole thing over a package of Chinese noodles. One favorite was chili pie, prepared by putting Fritos in an oven-proof casserole adding a chopped onion and a can of chili with beans, topping with cheddar cheese, and baking until bubbling. Though that style of cooking is long gone, I appreciated the recipes and Margaret's thoughtfulness in sending them.

Knox Jr.'s arrival demanded more adjustments, getting up in the middle of the night to nurse, trying not to wake Knox who needed his sleep for all the work he had to do. But I loved being Knox's wife and Knox Jr.'s mother, and we were very happy with each other and with our wonderful son. It seemed magical to have made such a perfect baby. Our finances put limitations on us but we were in the same situation as most of his classmates and we knew we could look forward to better times.

CHAPTER 7
THE BAPTISM AND THE BLUE ALBUM

Knox Jr. was a happy baby, and Knox, proud of his son, decided to have him baptized and show him off to his mother and family in Texas. Perhaps his desire for a baptism was also one of those "old records" that keeps playing in our minds, suggesting the right things to do and the right way to do them. I knew that Knox was beginning to question his fundamentalist background, and while I'm unsure about my own beliefs at that time, I certainly was unaware that baptism meant that we were agreeing to raise Knox Jr. in the Presbyterian Church. But Knox spoke as if everything had already been decided.

"We could fly out before Christmas. Uncle Julian could perform the ceremony in Brownwood and then we could spend the holiday with mother in Sherman. The Texas family could meet the baby. Mother would love it."

Unprepared for this declaration, I hardly knew what to say. I objected that we might be tempting fate, flying with an infant on a plane crowded with contagious strangers. I knew we didn't have the money; since I had quit work we were barely scraping by. But Knox had it all worked out. Although he hadn't told me, he could get a lab job his last year in medical school, which would bring in a little extra money. And to calm my fears about Knox Jr. getting sick, he reminded me that nursing babies acquire their mother's immunities. It was settled. Christmas week, we would fly to Texas.

We arrived in Sherman, where Knox's mother met us at her home. She was happy to see Knox, and as her eyes lit up looking at the baby it seemed as if a veil lifted from her face; for a moment she looked pretty and even happy. Then she greeted me politely and began showing us around the house.

When I stepped through the front door, I could smell artichokes cooking and immediately recalled the encounter when she had demanded my reasons for wanting to marry her son. My anxiety escalated. Even though I been unable to express my love for Knox then, surely now she could see how we loved one another. Knox, busy trying to coax a smile out of Knox Jr., did not notice my apprehension.

Margaret's house was plain, comfortable, and orderly. In the living room she had set out a collection of Hummel figurines and on the sideboard stood some pewter pieces and a large copper vessel, which Knox said his parents had bought in Europe during W. K.'s sabbatical from Harvard. There were no paintings or pictures on the walls and no photographs on the mantel or the tables. This did not seem to be the home of a woman who invited friends over for a casual meal or a cup of coffee, but, after all, Margaret was a full-time social worker and, as she made it known, she didn't have time for entertaining or other "extras."

We got our instructions. We would drive to Brownwood, some 250 miles away, where we would stay with family friends who lived across the street from Grandmother Chandler. We would have dinner at grandmother's after the service. Knox's aunts Bettie and Meggs would be there, and of course Uncle Julian, Meggs' husband, who would perform the baptism.

Margaret offered us a cold drink and pulled out a gift for the baby, a very nice two-piece blue outfit. It was too small, but she assured us that we could exchange it, though unfortunately when I took it back to the shop, there wasn't a larger size or anything else appropriate. When I relayed this information to Margaret, she looked at me strangely and gave me money to buy him something in Louisville. I thought she might be disappointed because she had planned for Knox Jr. to wear her gift at the baptism, but the incident seemed insignificant and I forgot about it. Back in Louisville, I bought something for Knox Jr. and wrote Margaret a note thanking her.

The day of the baptism Knox Jr. would not settle down. Nursing him was difficult, since he had discovered a new game, bearing down on the nipple, then pulling away while still biting down. When he cut his first tooth the game had become more painful and I had little patience with his new entertainment. The baptism, dinner at Grandmother Chandler's, and an afternoon of socializing with family and neighbors lay ahead of us. Since I was nursing him by demand, I would have to find quiet places to retreat; these churchgoing relatives had made it clear to me that nursing in public was impolite at best, possibly even immoral.

I wanted to talk to Knox about my discomfort and my reaction to his mother, who followed me from room to room, standing behind me and watching as I tended to Knox Jr., but he was sure that Margaret was only interested in what I was doing. I hoped so, but I felt that my mother-in-law thought that I was not doing things the way she would have done them.

Knox tried to reassure me, putting his hands on my shoulders.

"Caroline, don't be silly. I'm positive that she thinks you are wonderful. That's just her way."

I wanted to get along and be a good daughter-in-law, but things didn't seem to be going well. I could have used a hug right then. But Knox, struggling with his tie, hurried us along.

"We don't want to be late," he said.

⌣

Knox proudly held his son in his arms as we mingled with the town folk in front of the Southern Presbyterian Church. The Texan greetings were warm.

"That's a strappin' fellow ya got there."

And "They treatin' ya right up there?"

Or, a warning, "Ya know that too much book learnin' will ruin a good man."

The inside of the church resembled every other Presbyterian church I had attended. Dark pews with burgundy-colored cushions, colored glass windows depicting New Testament images, and a raised podium for the minister. We were seated near the front. The service included a sermon by Knox's uncle, the Reverend Julian Sleeper. I'm afraid that my mind was not on what he said but on the people who had come to see Knox Jr.'s baptism, and of course I was keeping my eye on the five-month-old clinging to his father's arm. He looked as cute as ever, but I could tell by his expression that he wasn't happy among so many unfamiliar people, and he didn't seem to like sitting in a pew looking at people's backs.

The next thing I knew, Uncle Julian had descended from the pulpit and gestured for us to come forward to the baptismal font. He read the prescribed words, something about our promise to raise Knox Jr. in the "house of the Lord," which made me uncomfortable; Knox Jr. looked at me with pleading eyes, as uncomfortable as I was. Knox lowered him closer to the font, and as Uncle Julian's hand scooped up water from the font, the splash flew off his fingers onto the baby's face. We heard a heart-rending scream followed by a wailing cry, which caused my milk to come in so copiously that it soaked the entire front of my blouse. I wanted to be anywhere but there. Instead, I reached out, gathered up the screaming baby, and held him against my milk-soaked chest. Margaret stood there, looking at me with an expression of disbelief, saying nothing. Just looking.

As we left the church, I said that I'd have to change my blouse before going to the family dinner.

"We don't have time," Knox said. "You're fine."

"I don't think so," I said shifting the baby off my chest. He agreed, quickly.

⌣

After a quick detour to change my blouse, we arrived at Grandmother Chandler's house only a few minutes late. Knox's grandmother, a pretty, youthful-looking woman in her seventies with an innate dignity, came out to the porch, greeted me warmly, clucked over Knox Jr., and drew me into the house.

I instantly felt at home. The living room was bright and airy, with light-colored curtains framing the windows, sofas and chairs arranged for conversation, and a table set up for family card games. Photos and knickknacks stood on the tables, and the cinnamon smell of apple pie wafting from the kitchen took me back to my childhood visits to my dad's family in rural Kentucky. Knox's two paternal aunts came out from the kitchen, wiping their hands on their aprons. Aunt Meggs, the younger sister, gave us buxom hugs and immediately reached for the baby, who happily stretched out his arms to her. Aunt Bettie, reserved by comparison, smiled as she took in Knox's young family.

As we chatted about inconsequential things, my earlier apprehension faded. Knox's mother and Aunt Bettie joined Grandmother Chandler out in the kitchen. I could hear the pans rattling, and with a pang of guilt wondered if I should be helping, but before I could decide, Aunt Meggs came over and sat down beside me.

Brownwood, Christmas 1958
Front row: Margaret, Aunt Meggs, Knox Jr., and Carrie
Back row: Knox, Caroline, and Uncle Julian

"Knox Jr. reminds me of his grandfather," she said. "Something in his smile, I think. But he is also a lot like your Knox was as a child. You know we called him 'Pachy' because he was big, like a pachyderm. And outgoing, a little devilish." She paused. "My brother, Knox's father, was not as outgoing."

Aunt Meggs hesitated, as if the memories of her brother were about to bring tears to her eyes. "No, I think

Knox Jr. is more like your husband, the second Knox."

I was surprised to be talking about Knox's father in such a natural way, especially since I had met Meggs only moments before. No one else, not even my husband, had talked much about him, and certainly not so intimately.

"You know, I have never seen a picture of Knox's father. I have no idea what he looked like," I said, turning to Aunt Meggs.

As soon as I spoke, I realized I might have said the wrong thing. But surely it was all right to ask, especially since, as far as I could tell, neither his mother, his widow, or his son, seemed to have a photo of him. Aunt Meggs jumped up and ran out of the room, startling Knox Jr. with her hasty exit. She came back with a large, blue album, its front cover embossed in gold, and placed it on the sofa beside me, reaching out again for the baby.

I have often thought that the photos in a family album reveal much more than the passage of time. I looked around; Knox was engaged in conversation with Aunt Meggs and Knox Jr. was content being jiggled on her lap. I had a few moments to sneak a look into the family of the man I had married. I picked up the cumbersome album and set it on my lap, thrilled with the opportunity to see what Knox's father looked like. Though I was just leafing through a photo collection, somehow the moment seemed portentous. The photos were not tucked into adhesive photo corners, but carefully arranged under plastic and permanently glued down, as if they were being saved for posterity.

Pious-looking ancestors stared out from the first few pages: Sarah Williams who married William Alexander Knox Jr. and produced six children, one of whom was Carrie, grandmother Chandler.

Later photos showed her with her husband, Samuel Ezekiel Chandler (S. E. Chandler), the fundamentalist preacher, father of W. K., Bettie, and Meggs. And while there were four pages of Knox family photos, there were only two pictures of the Chandlers, a single portrait of S.E.'s father Ezekiel and a faded tintype of his wife Isabelle. All the photos had been taken by professional photographers, the subjects formally posed.

Later on came a group portrait, taken around 1916 and labeled "Knox Reunion—Dime Box." At first I thought Dime Box was the type of camera used for the photo, but I later learned that Dime Box, Texas, was the site of the reunion.

Other photos showed Carrie and her five siblings, all of whom, including the three girls, had graduated from the University of Texas. A group shot showed three generations decked out in their Sunday best, ready for a ride in a magnificent convertible Model T Ford, a 1908-10 double seater. On the next page, I found the first picture of W. K., taken when he was about four years old, standing with his two sisters and three cousins in front of a large Victorian house in Corpus Christi. The children were formally dressed, except for W. K., who was barefoot and in shorts, maybe shirking convention even at an early age.

W. K. was clearly a much loved and admired child.

Top: *Knox family reunion, Dime Box, 1916*
W. K. is seated in the front row, second from right.
Bottom: *The Knox family, 1910*

W. K. with sisters and cousins, 1904

Photos displayed him as a chubby baby, a toddler, a teenager, a young Army recruit, and a professor. As a young adult, he was handsome with piercing dark eyes, often sporting a mischievous smile. As I stared at a close-up, the distance between us seemed to shrink and I traveled back to the past, seeing him in carefree moments—picnicking, swimming, taking target practice. In my imagination I joined the girls enjoying the new freedoms of the Roaring Twenties—driving, smoking, voting, reaching toward equality with the boys. Meggs, wholesome, outgoing, and modern even in her nickname, posed in a flapper dress and a rakish straw hat. The men looked stylish in riding britches, fedoras, Panama hats, or caps. The photos suggested that Meggs and W. K. had been close, that he

W. K., Meggs, and friends in Texas, c. 1917

had enjoyed good times and good friends, and that he was comfortable with the equality and certainly the company of women. I would have liked to have known him.

The last photo of W. K., taken at Thanksgiving in 1942, probably home on leave from the OSS, showed him with Margaret, his sister Bettie, his parents and Colston. Meggs had lovingly pieced together a chronicle of the first two William Knox Chandlers—W. K., born in 1900, and my husband, Knox born in 1933. The third William Knox Chandler, my son Knox Jr., born in 1958, was at the moment squirming in her lap. The sense of continuity I got from the album thrilled me and I felt included in a large, happy family.

I turned another page. Something fell from the back of the album onto the floor—the only thing that hadn't been firmly glued down. I leaned over to pick it up, ready to tuck it back into the book. It was a clipping from the *Chicago Sun*, mildewed and yellowed. My eyes were drawn to a close-up of a young woman under whose pretty face ran the caption "Rosemary Sidley, former Chicago society girl, who was fatally wounded by William Knox Chandler, a suitor, in her Washington, D.C., home. Chandler then killed himself."

Stunned and unbelieving, I read the caption again more slowly. Rosemary Sidley, a former society girl, murdered by William Knox Chandler. I couldn't finish the article. Unable to fully understand what I had just read, I sat there frozen on the sofa, trying to compose myself, remaining motionless maybe for a few minutes, maybe

The last photo of W. K. with his family, Brownwood, Thanksgiving 1942

longer. I didn't think my husband knew about the murder since he had never even hinted at it, though maybe it was a family secret like my mother's alcoholism, something Knox knew but wouldn't speak about. Clearly I couldn't bring it up during the celebration of Knox Jr.'s baptism, so I stuffed the clipping back into the album.

For a few minutes, sensing a bond with Meggs and captivated by the photographs, I had felt part of the Chandler family from which Margaret's cool reserve excluded me, but the shocking newspaper article shattered that feeling of belonging. I forced myself to look back at the album. The last two pictures of W. K. showed him as scholar, lecturing at Radcliffe College in 1939 (see page 27) and then sitting casually in an easy chair surrounded by his books and papers, smiling as he worked at home. I thought back to the Thanksgiving photo from 1942, the last family photo that includes W. K.

To get through the rest of the day, I had to pretend that I hadn't seen the article. I set the Blue Album carefully on a table and leaned back on the sofa, closing my eyes and trying to forget what I wished I had never seen.

That evening back at Margaret's house, confused and disturbed by my discovery, I ached for all of them, for W. K.'s mother, for his sisters, and for Knox and Colston who had grown up without a father. Yet it was Margaret, left alone to bring up her two children, for whom I felt the greatest sympathy. The thought that W. K. had betrayed her with another woman and then murdered the woman and himself must have tormented Margaret for years.

W. K. in his Cambridge study, 1939

CHAPTER 8
LOUISVILLE TO BETHESDA

Back in Louisville Knox continued to follow a demanding schedule, completing his last year of medical school courses, taking physics classes on campus, doing research with Dr. Rehm, and continuing with the lab work that had paid for our flights to Texas. I rarely saw him and was often lonely. From time to time my mind wandered back to the Blue Album, and the burden of my knowledge of the murder and the "other woman" began to weigh on my conscience. If Knox didn't know the whole story and if I didn't tell him about the article, I would be harboring a secret, doing something contrary to what I believed made for an honest relationship in marriage. Intuitively I did not think that Knox knew more about his father's death than the sketchy details he had mentioned, because he seemed too honest in his acceptance of himself to conceal something as important as the murder-suicide. I could also understand his mother's reasons for secrecy, her desire to shield the boys from the ugly truth while they were young, even if keeping silent meant denying them memories of their father. The implied relationship headlined in the newspapers was too painful for her to talk about, almost too painful to bear. Perhaps the rest of the family remained silent out of shame, but they may have been pulled into a conspiracy to keep the Secret from the boys. I wondered especially about Aunt Meggs. When she handed me the Blue Album, did she recall she had put the article inside? Did she want me to know the whole truth, to have her brother remembered even though the memory pained her? The photographs of W. K. continued to haunt me: pictures of a fine, intelligent man, a husband, father, son and brother whose existence had been completely erased—except for some photos and a yellowed clipping in a sister's Blue Album.

And still I hesitated to tell Knox about the article, giving myself all sorts of excuses. The news might be psychologically calamitous. His grand-father S. E. Chandler had been sent away for a "rest" while president of Daniel Baker College, and the family believed that W. K. had had some kind of a breakdown before killing himself. Perhaps my husband had inherited this familial tendency to emotional fragility. Although everything I knew about Knox indicated that he was strong, stable, and secure, I began to wonder whether I really knew him. Or myself? I had entered into marriage with little sense of my own identity, something that perhaps Knox's mother saw when she challenged my motives for wanting to marry her son. I had been brought up to do what was "proper" and "right," and so I was thinking not only about what was good for Knox and me, but also about the possible repercussions of revealing the Secret; telling him of the murder would open an ugly can of worms. I was afraid to do anything, afraid to say anything, afraid to open the can. I decided to hold off telling Knox about the murder; after all, graduation was only a few months away and breaking the news might spoil the big occasion. Without realizing it, I had already joined the Chandler family's conspiracy of silence.

———

In the fall, after Knox graduated, we would head for the National Institutes of Health (NIH) where he would join the Public Health Service and work with Kenneth S. Cole, Kacy to his friends, whom Dr. Rehm had suggested as a mentor. Dr. Cole is recognized today as the father of biophysics, and his research on electrical resistance in nerve cells, which had formed the basis for progress in neurophysiology during the 1930s and 1940s, would influence the path of Knox's career. Knox flew to Bethesda for an interview.

After the meeting, which went well, Knox was waiting for a taxi to the airport when a black man pulled up and offered him a ride. Knox hesitated for a moment, trying to decide whether to get into the back seat or the passenger seat next to the driver. He decided on the front seat, and the two men enjoyed a pleasant exchange of thoughts and ideas as they drove. Knox had never experienced a meaningful conversation with a black person before, and the encounter brought home to him the racial baggage of his Southern upbringing. Later when he recounted the story, tears would come to his eyes and he would sometimes find it difficult to finish.

When Knox Jr. was almost nine months old, I became pregnant with our second child, disproving the belief that nursing protects women from pregnancy. When Great Aunt Libbut, who had taken care of Knox back in Tuleta, Texas, heard the news, she hastily posted a letter telling him to seek advice about birth control at the medical school. We smiled at the implications of her suggestion, but were happy to be providing Knox Jr. with a playmate close in age.

Margaret came to Louisville for Knox's graduation, and we shared our pride in him, knowing how hard he had worked and how brilliantly he had succeeded.

Knox's graduation from University of Louisville Medical School, 1959

Although she said nothing directly, her pleasure shone in her eyes when she looked at her son, just as it did when she looked at Knox Jr. While she didn't seem eager to hug and kiss her grandson, she was a loving grandmother, reading stories and helping him with the usual toddler challenges. She also appeared to be a good mother and a good enough mother-in-law. I promised myself to work on building our relationship, and to embrace her and to include her in our family.

Margaret, Knox Jr., and Knox after the graduation, 1959

In the fall of 1959 we left Louisville for the NIH, a sad departure for my father, but a relief for me since my mother's unpleasant alcohol-induced behavior was in full bloom again. Although going to Bethesda removed me from daily contact with her, it did not free me from the kind of abusive drunken phone calls I had received at college. She remained in denial, maintaining that there was nothing wrong with her, but years later I realized that dad, my brother, and I had enabled her alcoholism by remaining silent, never even bringing up the subject.

⌣

Our first Maryland home was a rental in the "Luxury Apartments" in Rockville, a few miles from the NIH and the Navy Hospital complex. Its "luxury" was confined to its name; our own furnishings remained absolutely basic—except for the wedding gifts which we carefully unpacked and arranged in a dry sink we had bought for the purpose. In December our darling Janet was born at the Navy Hospital, only moments after our arrival, because Knox stopped for gas and then waited patiently for the attendant to count out the green reward stamps we had earned for our purchase.

Before Knox's mother and brother joined us for Christmas, we received a disturbing letter from Aunt Bettie telling about a "falling-out" with Margaret. Bettie enclosed a copy of her own reply to Margaret, which pleaded for reconciliation over what Bettie thought was a misunderstanding. Grandmother Chandler had willed her house to Bettie and Meggs with the understanding that they would even up the bequest financially with Margaret, their brother's widow, who already had her own house. Bettie's letter explained her feelings:

> Dear Margaret,
> Your letter absolutely stunned me. We had no idea you thought we were trying 'to beat you and the boys' out of anything, as Meggs told you that night, we would see that it would be evened up financially. Your accusations have stunned and grieved me so. I have always loved you dearly and been so proud of the way you came through your terrible trouble. It seems that it must be a nightmare that you have misjudged me so and don't even want an explanation...

In a second letter to Knox, Bettie added that when the three women had met for the reading of the will, Margaret had not shown distress or resentment, but had kissed Bettie and Meggs goodbye as usual. Actually Margaret did not trust Bettie and Meggs to give her the third of the inheritance to which the will entitled her, and thus she believed the two were cheating Margaret's sons out of their share. Bettie's letter assuring her that they would make it up to her financially did not lessen Margaret's conviction that she was being wronged. What the sisters considered a misunderstanding, Margaret saw as a major breach of trust. She simply cut off communications.

Knox and I did not know how to process the information. We understood that his mother mistrusted her sisters-in-law and would not discuss with them the reasons for her resentment, but we were inclined to think the three could iron out their differences, and so we did not bring up the issue during Margaret's Christmas visit. Although we never found out whether she reconciled with Bettie and Meggs, we did learn that she received her third of the estate, which she divided between Knox and Colston. Knox gave his share to our children, embarrassed by the whole incident. Looking back, we realized that it was only one of many disagreements between Margaret and her relatives, usually over money or to do with her sense of being treated unjustly by others.

⌣

During our two years in Rockville we spent the summers at the Marine Biological Laboratory at Woods Hole on Cape Cod. There Knox spent long hours in the laboratory, observing experiments the first year and the following summer working on a project measuring impedance in single squid nerve cells. I took the children to the beach and enjoyed adult conversation with the other mothers.

Margaret visited us in 1961 when Colston

graduated from Brown University. We were getting along well and she continued enjoying her grandmotherly activities, reading to the children and selecting thoughtful gifts for them, though remaining physically standoffish. My own mother, at least when in her "Fairy Godmother" mode, would get down on the floor with her grandchildren and shower them with hugs and kisses. I asked Knox if his mother had ever been affectionate when he was a little boy, hugging and kissing him or holding him.

"I don't remember anything like that," he answered. "But it doesn't mean that she didn't when I was really young. She is reserved, Caroline."

I knew that she was reserved, but her lack of physical affection for the children still seemed strange. Since I was getting vibes from Knox that I should back off, I dropped the subject.

⌣

That same year, after Knox returned from the first international biophysics meeting in Stockholm, he decided that he needed more coursework in applied mathematics and physical chemistry. So after our two years at the NIH, we moved to Providence where he held a fellowship at Brown University.

I liked Providence. When I had visited the Rhode Island School of Design (RISD) my senior year in high school, the high level of student work had impressed me. While I could visualize myself there, I knew without asking that my father, who wanted me to have a liberal arts background and a traditional college experience, would disapprove of such a "hippie school." I obeyed his wishes, but never forgot that visit, which in retrospect seemed to represent my destiny to enter the art world.

At Goucher I had enjoyed two painting classes that introduced modern concepts in art. Now, in Providence, practically in the shadow of RISD, my desire to paint reawakened—though maybe I just needed a night out. Since Knox could babysit while he studied at home during the evenings, I signed up for a figure painting class with Herman Itchkawitch, a local teacher connected with RISD. Although I was hoping to work in the style of van Gogh, Mr. Itchkawitch approached figure painting in the manner of Rembrandt, a stretch for me, but I worked hard, telling myself that I had to learn to paint realistically in order to leave realism behind. Mr. Itchkawitch was a good teacher, and if I could have stayed with him, he might have led me toward what I was seeking. We bought one of his beach scenes, a modern, mysterious, unfinished piece that I still admire. "Unfinished" art has long fascinated me because it is interactive: what the painter has "left out" allows space for the viewer's imagination to wander. I feel that I could walk along that lonely uncompleted beach.

⌣

In 1962 Knox received a post-doctoral fellowship to work in Cambridge, England, with Alan Hodgkin and Richard

Adrian, two distinguished British physiologists. Knox felt honored with the opportunity, and we both looked forward to living abroad, though I was pregnant with our third child and apprehensive about giving birth in another country. I was also disappointed at giving up my painting classes. We sorted through our belongings deciding what to take with us, what to throw out, and what to put in storage. We stored the unused wedding silver, china, and crystal, but I carefully packed my art supplies.

CHAPTER 9
TO ENGLAND

Our Atlantic crossing on the *Statendam* was luxury itself, with a well-appointed cabin, a swimming pool, a shuffleboard court, and entertainment for the children, as well as delicious meals in the dining room. Unfortunately, I was seasick for the entire week, but I was happy that my queasiness gave Knox the opportunity to bond with Janet and Knox Jr.

In Cambridge we settled in at #2 Petersfield, a row house on a small park called Donkey's Common. The house had been condemned for dry rot, but it still had two major pluses: it was an easy walk to the center of Cambridge, and it breathed a certain historic charm. I enjoyed living in a house connected architecturally to other people, and even though the neighbors weren't outgoing, it was pleasant to see them in the yards adjacent to ours.

The liabilities of #2 Petersfield far outweighed its advantages. It lacked central heating, so that keeping warm became a complicated, labor-intensive effort, each room with its own heating device that demanded its own kind of attention. The sitting room had a coal stove with a fan to move the hot air, the dining area had a Rayburn cook stove also fired by coal, and the front parlor had a coal fireplace. One room featured a coin-operated gas heater (which Rie Stieger, our Danish au pair, who acquired a Southern accent while living with us, called a "gah-us fi-er"). In the

Knox with Knox Jr. and Janet, #2 Petersfield, 1962

bathroom two Aladdin kerosene heaters supplemented an inadequate 12-inch electric wall heater mounted six feet above the floor. In the bedrooms 500-watt electric heaters, roughly equivalent to five light bulbs, struggled to take the edge off the chill, while in the master bedroom a large cage-like device with a 100-watt bulb attached inside was intended to dry the damp bedcovers during the day.

The second drawback of #2 Petersfield was its lack of refrigeration, a larder taking the place of a refrigerator. Grocery shopping became a daily chore, especially since I had only a bicycle for transportation. On days when there was no pre-school, I pedaled along with Janet on a seat in front of me and Knox Jr. perched on one behind as our third child grew bigger every day inside me. On the way home, the groceries dangled from the handlebars in multiple string bags.

The third drawback of #2 Petersfield was its subterranean atmosphere. Several of the rooms—the kitchen, larder, and coal storage room—were half underground, so that we cooked, ate, and dealt with the laundry in damp, dark rooms whose windows opened high on the walls. Since I had grown up in a house where the basement was mysterious and off limits, living underground was psychologically difficult for me.

⌣

I had waited to purchase maternity clothes in England and was told that the local maternity shop was "a bicycle ride out from town." I rode the seven miles out from Cambridge to find only a small, sparsely outfitted store. When I asked for maternity clothes, the clerk shook her head. "They are out of season," she said. Either my shocked look or my American accent gave me away, but the saleswoman added helpfully, "You make do with a large jumper, dearie. You will find them at Marks and Spencer.

A "jumper" turned out to be a sweater. But when I couldn't find one I liked in Cambridge, a salesgirl gave me the address of a "knitting lady," who could make one that would surely suit me and, she added, might even be cheaper. She was right. The hand-knit, turquoise mohair sweater was perfect and no more expensive than the store-bought jumper. It did cover up the evidence of pregnancy though it made me look enormous. To complete my wardrobe I stitched up—by hand—a brown and a black maternity tunic, which I wore with a variety of shirts and leggings, on top of which I donned the grey overcoat I had brought from home.

In spite of help from a cleaning lady and Rie, my daily schedule demanded the energy of a dervish and the stamina of a marathoner. While Rie took Knox Jr. and Janet to pre-school, I set off grocery shopping on the bicycle. At 12:30 Knox came home for the big midday meal and returned to the lab afterwards. I did household chores until 4:30 when we had tea, actually the children's supper, then with Rie's help bathed the children, read to them, and put them to bed, in time to prepare Knox's supper at 7:30, after which he returned to the lab until late in the evening. I soon realized that having time to paint was a total pipe dream.

In spite of this hectic routine, Knox and I found Cambridge itself delightful. He could not have been happier with his position in the laboratory with Alan Hodgkin. I told myself I would adjust to all the inconveniences with good humor and get back to the painting later.

Shortly after we had settled in at #2 Petersfield, Knox informed me that he would be going with the rest of the people in Alan's lab to the Marine Biological Laboratory in Plymouth, some 300 miles away on the southwest coast of England, where he would observe experiments on squid nerve fiber. When he told me that the children and I would not be joining him, I failed to muster up much good humor. The lab with its roster of eminent scientists was a plum opportunity for Knox, but I felt insecure about being left behind in a cold, damp house, with no close friends and only a bicycle for transportation. Knox listened, but replied that he had to go and that I could not. Fortunately this time the stay in Plymouth was only a few weeks.

Looking back, I realize how protected my life had been and how afraid I still was of being alone, as afraid as I had been in Louisville when Knox went off to the bachelor party. I later asked Dorothy Meves, whose husband Knox had come to know in Plymouth, how she had managed to accompany him to Plymouth, and though we became good friends I never did learn her secret. When I asked Alan Hodgkin's wife, she replied, "I would not be caught dead in Plymouth."

Our third child, Cara, joined us the end of January. I knew before we left the States that the baby would be delivered by natural childbirth, without the drugs and spinal block of my first two deliveries. I had been led to believe that the birth would take place at home, but we discovered that I could have the baby in the hospital if we could get one of Cambridge's two obstetricians to attend. We chose Miss Bottomly (surgical specialists in England go by Mr. or Miss). I did well, though the delivery was not easy, and we were thrilled when the nurses placed our precious eight-pound Cara on my stomach to rest while they served tea, a wonderful way to bond.

"A ginger-headed poppet," said the nurses. "We will let the wee one rest before we clean her up." Because I had help at home, Cara came home with us the next day, but did not leave our bedroom for a month because the rest of the house was too cold.

—

Knox's work with Alan Hodgkin was going so well that we were to stay on in Cambridge a second year, a prospect that became more appealing because we could move to a better house. The house on Cavendish Avenue had a small electric refrigerator with a freezer that held two ice cube trays and a washing machine that I could pull up to the sink. The primitive clothes dryer was a wooden frame with a fabric hood that fit over an electric heater on the floor; depending on the weather the clothes dried in perhaps one or two days. Because we were farther out from town, we bought a second-hand Morris Oxford, a luxury, and we even had a "telly."

Though the Cavendish Avenue house put Petersfield to shame in terms of mod cons, it lacked the

Knox in Alan Hodgkin's lab, 1963

charm of our former home. The décor was fussy; the furniture was covered in printed fabric and the walls almost completely obscured with paintings that expressed the "French" tastes of the owner. I took down the paintings and stored them away, which made the rooms less claustrophobic.

During the summer Knox and I traveled to Italy, where I saw works of art that I had never dreamed I would actually see, and we wined and dined ourselves nightly. The second winter Knox again went to Plymouth, this time to participate rather than just observe. Soon after he arrived, Alan learned that he had won the Nobel Prize and would return to Cambridge, which meant that Knox would be working with Richard Adrian and Hans Meves instead of Alan. I surprised myself with how well I handled his long absence, but I had become more accustomed to life in Cambridge and had made a friend or two.

The second summer Knox and I vacationed in France, which we enjoyed until a telegram arrived, informing us that Cara had had a seizure. We drove straight through to Cambridge, sharing the driving. Cara had come down with a sore throat; the sitter had not been able to get her to drink anything, and she had become dehydrated. I worried that the seizure might permanently affect her and blamed myself because I knew that *I* would have been able to get her to swallow liquids. The incident reawakened my maternal guilt for putting my own pleasure above my children's well-being.

The third winter Knox went to Plymouth again, this time, finally, to work with Alan. I was happy for him, even if it meant another English winter in a cold house, though Knox Jr.'s enthusiasm for carrying in the coal made the season more enjoyable. I was pregnant again, facing another English childbirth. In April, Margaret was born in the Evelyn Nursing Home, like Cara a wonderful ginger-headed poppet.

With our lives happy and full, I began planning our return to the States, looking forward to a place of our own with central heating and maybe even a dishwasher. Knox,

Hans Meves and Knox in Alan's lab, 1963

however, had something else in mind. One night after the children were in bed and we were sitting by the fire with a glass of wine, he broached the subject. He began talking cautiously about going home and then, with impeccable timing, introduced an alternative.

"I know that you have had your heart set on going back," he said, "but Alan has worked out a way that we could stay on."

Before I could open my mouth he added, "Now don't say anything until you have thought it over. It would mean so much to me and my career."

There it was again. The conflict between what I wanted and what was best for Knox professionally. After three years I was unhappy with staying on in the most patriarchal society that I had ever experienced, where women by definition were second-class citizens. Knox and Richard Adrian would go to banquets at the colleges, to which I was not invited; he would spend weeks in a lab at Plymouth, while I stayed at home. Excluded from social activities and left alone with the children for long periods of time, I felt cheated out of my dream of a close family and an intimate relationship with my husband, not one that seemed to be growing more and more distant. I had not liked the idea of staying on the third year, but I had done so, and now Knox was talking about staying on indefinitely.

Knox's grant ran out at the end of the academic year, and when I brought up the subject of money, he looked as if he hoped I wouldn't mention the topic.

"Alan thought he could get me a junior faculty position that would pay about half of what we are living on, maybe as much as $5,000."

I could barely manage the words, "Five thousand a year?"

But his expression said he meant exactly that. I hadn't seen my family for three years; my parents had never seen Cara or Margi and had missed out on a lot with

Knox Jr. and Janet. We were scrimping already and could not afford to live on half our present income. If the offer had been reasonable, I don't think I could have stood in Knox's way. I did appreciate what Cambridge had offered us and I know that Knox was grateful for the opportunities my willingness to live there had given him. But the anti-feminism of British academia and the adjustments to life on the home front sorely tested my vow not to stand in the way of Knox's science.

We set out for America to pick up the lives we had left behind in 1962. We were going back to Bethesda, and Knox was going back to the NIH.

CHAPTER 10
RETURNING HOME

Back in the States in 1965, we rented a split-level house near the NIH in Ashburton, a section of Bethesda, Maryland. Although Ashburton with its English-inspired name and tidy brick houses was a cut above many of the suburban tracts developed after World War II, the split-level house turned out to be as difficult in its way as the old-fashioned English houses we had rented in Cambridge. Architecturally the Ashburton house expressed the idea of "openness," something I applaud in relationships but not in floorplans. The house lacked privacy. When you entered the front door, you could look directly ahead through the living room into the dining room and the kitchen, or down into the recreation room, or up to the bedrooms. You could not find a quiet spot indoors unless all four children—and the dog—were outside. The house also lacked individuality, with every house in Ashburton identical to every other. Though Knox Jr. and Janet, walking home from school, soon learned which house was ours, at first they relied on the house number to distinguish it from its surrounding clones.

I had hoped that the three years in England, which had given me freedom from my mother's anger, might have softened her resentments, but the problems resurfaced on our first visit to Kentucky. Things went smoothly until one evening dad served bourbon during the cocktail hour;

mother kept on drinking during dinner and as the adults were having coffee, the "Wicked Witch" appeared once again, launching her accumulated grievances at me, in front of Knox. Here was the embarrassing moment I had long dreaded.

Mother dredged up an incident I barely remembered. "You didn't stop to see your Aunt Caroline on your way back from Florida which was why I let you have my car to make the trip."

"Please, don't do this," I begged, unaware that she had been nursing hurt feelings for seven years.

"You said that you would stop to see her and I didn't want you to go to her house in your beaten up old thing." She meant my Chevy. I tried to explain: we were late getting started; I was pregnant and traveling with a toddler. We had thanked mother for the loan of her car and apologized for not stopping to see Aunt Caroline; at the time I thought that she had understood. But she wasn't finished.

"You are so ungrateful. I do nice things for you and you don't appreciate them. You never have appreciated all that I have done for you. I didn't raise you to be selfish."

I knew that no amount of pleading would get her off the subject, so I excused myself from the table and went to bed. Knox could not understand why she directed her wrath at me and later, in our room, I confided that my mother had been angry with me for years and had always successfully masked her feelings until alcohol let her demons loose. Tomorrow she would not remember or at least acknowledge anything she had said. I understood that her resentment had to do with her disillusionment in my failing to become a Southern belle like my namesake Caroline Godfrey. I also believed that my supposed shortcomings reflected her disappointment in her own life.

But painful as the moment was, it brought some comfort. The "Wicked Witch" had appeared in front of my husband, yet the world did not end. Knox was understanding and supportive. I felt a wave of relief sharing this secret with him but, even so, ten years passed before I could say to anyone else "my mother is an alcoholic."

Soon after Knox started working at NIH, he announced that he had to return to Plymouth for three months to finish some experiments that he and Hans Meves had started. When we had come back to the States, I had not counted on Knox returning to England and leaving us behind.

Nevertheless during his absence, I threw myself into the role of American housewife, made friends with the neighbors, and basked in the conveniences of our split-level home. I enjoyed pushing the thermostat up and down instead of shoveling coal into a stove or lighting a kerosene heater. I enjoyed washing diapers in a machine and drying them in a dryer, instead of hanging them up outside where the coal dust in the air would turn them grey. But I did discover that American housewives were expected to have astonishingly high standards. Laundry was to be snowy white, bathrooms sparkling clean, and kitchen floors so shiny you could see your reflection in them, a finish achieved by repeated and conscientious applications of "Mop and Glo," whose name somehow concealed the effort involved.

The children, more English than American, had their own adjustments. When some of the neighborhood boys rang the doorbell asking Knox Jr. to join a baseball game, he could only answer, "I'd rah-thuh not," since he had no idea how to play the Great American Pastime. But, as children usually do, they adjusted comfortably. Cara, at two, did not have a large vocabulary, and what she had was all English: "biscuit" for cookie, "sweetie" for candy, and "nappies" for diapers. Nevertheless, she made her wishes known even if she didn't know the American words. The older children appreciated the open neighborhood where their friends could come and go at will instead of waiting to be invited for tea and relegated to the fenced-in back gardens for play.

⌣

Knox would return from England two days before Christmas, a holiday that would also bring Margaret, Colston, and his new wife Seeley to Ashburton. I wanted a festive American celebration, with a turkey, oyster stuffing, and cranberry sauce, stockings, a tree with electric lights and tinsel, and presents from Santa underneath, traditions we had not experienced for three years.

Although I looked forward to hosting the first Chandler reunion since Colston and Seeley were married, I was apprehensive since Margaret had not approved of Colston's marriage, even asking Knox to intervene because Seeley, "under the care of a psychologist," would "not make a stable candidate for marriage." Our crowded split level made living together difficult, but Knox as usual brought lightness to the household, which I desperately needed. Glad to have him back safe and sound, I tried to hide my unhappiness with his absence. Knox's mother seemed pleased to be with her children and grandchildren, including her namesake Margi, whom she had not previously met.

Things went fairly well until one evening after the children had been excused from the table and we sat chatting, mostly about Knox's experiences in England. I noticed Seeley talking quietly to Margaret and overheard her asking about Colston's dad, an innocent inquiry. Margaret clamped her jaw shut, rose from the table, and left the room, her body language shouting that Seeley had crossed a line. I felt sorry for my sister-in-law, who looked shocked that her effort to fit in the with family had met with such a negative response. How could she have known not to inquire about that man who would have been her father-in-law? But Margaret, without speaking, had enforced silence on the group, ending the conversation before it started.

As winter eased into spring, I sensed that Knox was not happy back at NIH. He rarely went into the lab, but worked in our bedroom, analyzing data from experiments he had done in England. I, too, felt gloomy. Our split-level house had become more an arena of disorganization than the tidy American home I had longed for during those years in England. An offer from Yale Medical School seemed an answer to our dreams.

Knox accepted, and we traveled to New Haven to look for housing. Fourteen miles east of the city, we discovered Guilford, a quaint New England town with an abundance of 18th- and 19th-century colonial houses.

My first sight of the serene and parklike town Green elated me: Guilford could be the place where we would raise our family, but after looking for days, we discovered that there were no rentals available and no houses we could afford to buy. Instead we found a rental in the Westville neighborhood of New Haven, the seventh place we had lived in our nine years of marriage; we would stay there until we saved the down payment for a house in Guilford.

Houses mean more to me, perhaps, than to other people, and I had long dreamed of a place that I would make into a home for my family. After the year of "open living" in

Ashburton, I realized that "my house" was more than something I dreamed of having, it was essential to my psychological well-being. My thinking about domestic spaces had been influenced by reading *The Poetics of Space* by the French philosopher Gaston Bachelard, who approached houses not as geometric spaces or historical artifacts, but as places with which we have a dynamic relationship. His analysis spoke about what we feel in different spaces, in closets or basements for example, how living in a certain house evokes our poetic imaginations. He had commented that "first you live in a house and then the house lives in you," which summed up my own sense that our houses hold our dreams and memories and in turn shape our emotional lives.

I thought back to the small spaces of my childhood, to the "house" under the dining room table covered with a blanket, which cut off everything else from view and allowed for a perfect make-believe world; or the closet that sheltered me as I hid from my drunken mother; to the caves that my brother and I dug out of the hillside for secret getaways, intimate comforting spaces. After Knox and I married and moved from town to town and house to house, it became increasingly clear that the spaces within the houses where I lived were important to me. Were they comforting or threatening, manageable or overwhelming, cozy and intimate, or cold and forbidding?

⌣

The apartment we rented in Westville for $165 a month was not the house I yearned for, but it had its attractions. It was spacious but also private: a 10-room duplex in a large stucco half-house with high ceilings, an outdated kitchen (by American, not English standards), an attic, a full basement, and a sun porch. The neighborhood offered playmates for the children and nearby schools; Knox could bicycle to work. Our stay in New Haven looked promising.

———

Before we had finished unpacking, Knox had to return to Texas to attend his grandmother's funeral, where he discovered that his mother had recently broken her leg. He phoned that he would bring Margaret home with him and that she would need a room on the first floor since she could not manage the stairs. The only option was the sun-room, so I ordered and installed blinds and brought in bedroom furniture. I realized that for the next few months I would be dealing not only with four children under eight who were adjusting to a new environment, but also with a mother-in-law on crutches. The weeks I spent caring for Margaret were made more difficult by her lack of appreciation, and I was about to throw in the towel when the orthopedist announced that her cast could come off. Long after she went back to Texas, I realized that her apparent lack of gratitude arose from her refusal to be indebted to anyone for anything, a trait that lasted her whole life.

I had not totally recovered from that visit when Margaret returned for the Christmas holidays. After breakfast while the children busied themselves with their new toys, we three adults sat around the table with another cup of coffee. Knox pulled out a letter he had received from Alan Hodgkin, asking him to come back to Cambridge for three months. Though I could see that Knox was truly honored by Alan's offer, I was shocked that he hadn't mentioned the invitation to me before bringing it up in front of his mother. Margaret beamed her approval, proud that her son had been asked by a Nobel laureate. The inevitability of his going to Cambridge quickly became apparent.

"We will all go, of course," I said. "We might have to make arrangements for the children to miss some school."

Knox reacted immediately.

"We can't afford for all of us to go." The issue was non-negotiable. Margaret continued smiling with maternal pride as she and Knox discussed Alan's offer, while I cleared the dishes, wondering how the two of them could not have at least a little sympathy for me. With hindsight, I am aware that I felt the need to be agreeable, to live up to my vow not to stand in the way of Knox's career, and to make the best of another separation. But I did not look forward to a summer without Knox, and it turned out to be worse than I had anticipated.

Summers in New Haven are always hot, but in the late 1960s, New Haven had been heating up in ways that had nothing to do with the weather. The city government had instituted an urban renewal plan that drastically changed the downtown. Urban planners demolished substandard housing and failing commercial areas, uprooting and relocating some 3,000 people, most of them poor, destroying whole neighborhoods in order to build a wide connector from the interstate highway to the center of town. The police responded to expressions of resistance—marches and picketing—by cracking down, arresting demonstrators, sometimes brutally. The mayor, Richard C. Lee, who excelled at garnering federal funds and became the face of urban renewal, also became the target of those who felt most abused by it.

Knox and I had been absent from the country for three years and while we had a sense of the major news events, we were basically out of touch. When we came back in 1965, we found a country in turmoil, with widespread demonstrations against the war in Vietnam and heightened tensions in the cities, including New Haven. In the summer of 1967, when Knox returned to England, riots erupted in Detroit, Newark, and New Haven. Inflammatory stories and rumors suggested that rioters were marching out toward the mayor's house in Westville, tossing torches into the houses along their way. For most of the three months that Knox was in Cambridge, I lay awake at night fearing that our house would be torched, repeatedly checking to see that windows were locked. For the first time in my life, I experienced paralyzing fear. Years later a neighbor who had been actively involved in the civil rights movement explained to me that I had no reason to fear the demonstrators; I should have talked to him in 1967, which would have helped put my mind at ease.

The third month of Knox's absence, Warren Rehm and his wife Barbara came to visit. Warren seemed to sense my suffering, which made it easy for me to express to him in a heart-to-heart talk after dinner that although I did not want to stand in Knox's way, my sacrifices seemed unending. I should have realized that Dr. Rehm's interests lay with Knox's career. He advised me to persevere: it was extremely important that Knox be allowed to do his research; Dr. Rehm knew from experience that scientists who couldn't accomplish what they had set out to do sometimes suffered psychological breakdowns.

So, if Dr. Rehm was correct, I was responsible for Knox's mental health; if he could not do what he felt he had to do and had a breakdown, it would be partly my fault. I had already worried about his psychological well-being if he found out the secret of his father's death, and now I was told he was in jeopardy if he did not succeed scientifically. Yet I also had a responsibility to the children. I realized I could not be a good mother if I didn't take better care of myself and I also thought they needed more attention from their father.

Knox returned, obviously pleased with the work that he had done with Alan Hodgkin and Richard Adrian on the electrical properties of frog muscle fiber. He had also enjoyed himself, living with the Hodgkins for the entire time, taking part in stimulating conversations and attending pleasant social gatherings, one of which included drinking wine out of old-fashioned rose petals in the famous gardens of a famous novelist. I wouldn't have denied him those experiences, but I wanted some for myself.

I decided that in the future we should make decisions together—without his mother being present. I didn't see other American scientists leaving their families for months at a time and I decided that I was not unreasonable in expecting more consideration and more of a voice in the marriage. I braced myself for an honest talk. I began by telling Knox that I knew it was an honor for him to work with Alan, an amazing opportunity to learn from such a prestigious scientist.

"However, I cannot go through this again," I said. "We must have a better understanding of what we can and cannot do in our relationship." I was trembling. "I will not stand for these long separations," I said. "I know that international phone calls are outrageously expensive and I didn't expect you to phone more often, but I did expect more letters. And Knox," I said almost on the verge of tears, "we all missed you... so very much."

Knox answered that he hadn't had any time alone, when he could write. He was always with Alan, at his house, eating with him, or in the lab working with him.

I understood that Alan required his undivided attention. "But two letters in three months?" I went on. "You don't seem to realize how hard it was, taking full responsibility for four little children with riots going on all summer." I added that I had been afraid to leave the windows open, even with the heat. "Can't you see my side of the situation," I finished.

His head lowered, he didn't answer. When he looked up, all he could say was "I'm sorry, I'm sorry, I'm really sorry."

I suspected that Knox at the time could not imaginatively put himself in my place. While he could be so careful to do the right thing, to be honest and fair in his dealings with others, he did not seem to have the ability to empathize with me. There was much about my husband and even more about my mother-in-law that I did not understand, but clearly I would have to say explicitly what I would and would not tolerate.

The notion that I would have to stand up for myself was an awakening, not easy when I had been schooled to accommodate to the needs of others. But that painful summer I realized that being a good wife and supporting Knox in his science did not mean that I had to martyr myself. For the first time I realized that my weakness in our relationship was a major part of the problem.

While I recognized that my inability to stand up for myself had contributed to my unhappiness, I continued to be bothered by my inability to tell Knox what I knew about his father. The silence Margaret had enforced on the rest of the Chandler family, now included me. Only Meggs, nine years ago at Knox Jr.'s baptism, had dared to break the code. Seeley had tried once, but been shut down rudely. If I am going to assert myself in this family, I asked myself, why shouldn't I ask about my husband's father? Yet, I waited 16 more years before Knox and I broached the topic with Margaret, and with disastrous results.

CHAPTER 11
GUILFORD

After two years in Westville, we began to look again for a house in Guilford—this time to buy. The town charmed me with its sense of history and its natural beauty. Settled in the 17th century as a farming community, it had remained remote enough from New Haven before the construction of the Connecticut Turnpike (now I-95) in the 1950s that many of its historic houses escaped destruction. At the center of town is the Green, which centuries ago served as common land for pasturing animals, burying the dead, and holding public ceremonies.

Although the earliest house in Guilford dates back to 1639 and there are several pre-Revolutionary houses, many of Guilford's historic homes were built in the Greek Revival style, which flourished between 1820 and 1860, a style that appealed to me for its classic proportions and its light-filled interiors.

In my imagination the beautiful historic houses on and around the Green had our family's image stamped on them, but they either were not for sale or were way beyond our means. The only affordable house that we liked at all was a few miles out from town on Goose Lane, an early road perhaps named for the wild geese that lived in the nearby salt marshes. The house had been built in the 19th century by farmers who had a plan of sorts, but little understanding of proportion or architectural detail.

Perhaps the builders had the Greek Revival style in mind, since the house had that general shape and was sited with the gable end facing the street, which emphasized the building's resemblance to a Greek temple. But it lacked the traditional Greek Revival details, for example the columns flanking the off-center front doorway. At some point it had been subdivided for two families, with kitchens on both floors and an outside staircase to the second story apartment. Unlike the spacious rooms in our Westville house, the nine rooms of the Goose Lane house were so small that the six of us could barely squeeze into any one of them. While it was not my dream house, the semi-rural neighborhood attracted us; it had enough land for Knox to plant a garden and for the children to keep animals.

As we were making up our minds, we noticed six-year-old Cara sitting on the ground next to the kitchen door, digging energetically in the dirt with a castoff serving spoon, oblivious to our presence. She stopped, looked at what she had done, and said with a great satisfaction, "I'm a fahm gurl"—as usual expressing her feelings succinctly. That clinched it. Although the house had many drawbacks, it was offbeat enough that we could transform it into our home. Knox and I smiled at Cara—so happy on her farm—and agreed to buy the house.

With the three older children in elementary school and Margi in nursery school, I began to repaint our nine little rooms, though I soon realized that paint alone could not make up for the house's fundamental shortcomings. Nor was this the kind of painting that I had been yearning for.

The route to Margi's nursery school took us along a country road in North Guilford past an old white farmhouse with green shutters. Across the road from the house stood a weathered red barn, a corncrib shaded with ancient maples, and a pasture where a few brown cows grazed peacefully behind a wooden fence. The house was classic Greek Revival except for a wing with a Victorian-style porch and an open carriage shed added to the left of the original house. The moment I saw it, the house spoke to me; it embodied my feelings for family and my sense of what domestic architecture should be. It was "my house," the house of my imaginings. I drove on by and dropped Margi off at her preschool.

When Margi entered elementary school, her "open classroom" kindergarten, with its freedom and hands-on learning inspired me to volunteer as a teacher's aide. I toyed with the thought of enrolling in an early childhood education program at Southern Connecticut State College and pursuing a teaching career. Our tight budget didn't include babysitters, but I could manage the evening classes if Knox took care of the children once a week during the dinner hour. I mentioned the possibility, but within two minutes of opening the discussion realized that he was not in favor of my taking the classes, in part because he and his colleagues were set to go with new research, about which he hadn't informed me.

"I won't be able to leave when we are in the middle of an experiment," he said, "and I can't tell how long an experiment will last. And, it's not a good idea to phone me at the lab because it might interfere with our work." If an experiment lasted beyond the children's dinner time, we were to eat without him. I recalled that our first date would take place "if the dog died." I also remembered that my mother had prophesied that waiting "for the dog to die," at least figuratively, would be the story of my life. I can't say that I hadn't been warned!

The academic requirement to publish or perish loomed large. To get tenure Knox had seven years to prove himself by publishing a significant number of noteworthy papers in scientific journals—preferably elite ones. When we had lived in Westville (and in England), he had returned to the lab after dinner, but Guilford was too far away. Aware of the pressure on him to design and perform high-quality experiments, analyze the data, write papers for publication, and submit applications for grants that would support his work financially, I knew I had to create time for him to work and I realized that I would have to drop my plans for my own career.

As I was trying to adjust to my disappointment, something wonderful happened; I heard about a local art teacher, Madeleine Sharrer, who taught figure-painting. I signed up for her Sunday afternoon session, which would not put too much strain on Knox, and from the first class, I realized that this was what I wanted.

Madeleine loved the work of Vincent van Gogh,

the flatness of his painting, his use of intense color and pattern, and his avoidance of perspective, modeling, and the interplay of light. To this approach she added her own vision of the world and the people in it, as well as her own symbolism. The moon became a compositional tool as well as a symbol of universal connection, even if it were painted red, green, or blue. Her intense colors were not just primary or secondary hues; she always added a bit of terre verte, earth green, to her tube paint—a little secret that she shared with me—which gave her pallet a personalized spectrum.

Madeleine lived in a stunning, barn-red, 18th-century, center-chimney colonial home. Before each class she sat in state in her living room, surrounded by sofas and pillows that were covered with patterned and many-hued fabrics imported from India and Japan. Her clothes of colorful, decorative fabrics repeated the exotic tone of the furnishings. I was where I wanted to be, in surroundings that spoke to me of Gertrude Stein and her 1920s atelier in Paris, an artistically and culturally stimulating and challenging atmosphere. I knew I had a lot to learn and that Madeleine had a lot to teach me.

I was also aware that my personal appearance fell short of Madeleine's standards, my wardrobe sorely neglected because of our financial situation. "Buy something beautiful," Madeleine would say, though I could barely afford the canvases, paint, and $30 monthly payments for the classes. But, determined, I knew I could make it work.

By good fortune an unusual job came my way—checking the town's open sludge pits, which were located down a dirt road across from our house. Guilford, rural in this respect, had no public sewage treatment system. "Honey wagons" pumped out the local septic systems and deposited the sludge in the pits. Dr. Elisabeth Adams, the local public health officer, coroner, and internist for all occasions, was charged with making sure that the pits did not overflow into the East River. From 1969 to 1971, not too proud to do a job that protected the environment and supported my art, I became Guilford's on-the-spot pit inspector. My wages, a dollar a day, paid the art class fee and made me more than happy; I was painting again.

On our four-acre "mini farm," Knox tended his garden; Knox Jr. raised chickens; we acquired lambs and geese, two of which made the mistake of decimating Knox's lettuce patch. He carried them in by their necks, his arms extended to keep them away from his body, mumbling something about having a "feather-pickin' tonight." Even after hours of cooking, they were still tough and, of course, the children absolutely refused to eat dinner.

Soon we outgrew the house and its tiny rooms. After some preliminary investigation into adding on to the house, I began asking around for available properties. A friend from North Guilford told me that no one ever moved away from there, so I was surprised when a week later she phoned back to say a house was about to come on the market and that I should contact a Carrie Edwards if I was interested. I phoned immediately.

Children at Goose Lane, 1968

Caroline followed by geese, 1970

Astonishingly, the Edwards' house was the Greek Revival about which I had developed such intense feelings merely by driving past it. I headed for North Guilford, shaking with anticipation.

The day was beautiful with the kind of blue sky that intensifies the reds and golds of the autumn maples, and I felt heady with the smell of the new-mown hay, the fragrance of the roadside wildflowers; even the aroma of cow manure wafting over from the barns somehow seemed attractive. I didn't know who owned the barn and corncrib across the street and I didn't care. It was the house that had my attention. As I pulled up in front, two cows stuck their heads over the fence, probably out of curiosity, but I took them as an omen, a welcoming party.

Carrie Edwards also welcomed me. Inside, the house seemed less spacious than it had appeared from the street. The galley kitchen was so small that I wondered how she had managed to cook for her large family in such a tight space. Beyond the kitchen were a modest dining room, a nice-sized living room, a front hall, and a front parlor. Upstairs were four bedrooms, one of them a walk-through. These shortcomings and the antiquated bathrooms were of no consequence. I declared the house "perfect"!

As I walked from room to room, the squeaky floors, the solid wooden doors, the two stairwells, the stone fireplace, the wavy glass in the windows, the uneven shed off the downstairs half bath, and the "three-holer" in the back yard clinched my decision. The house had a sense of mystery and the aura of history. I could not wait to tell Knox and the children that Carrie was prepared to sell for about the same price we would ask for the Goose Lane house, even though the North Guilford property came with two acres around the house and three-fourths of an acre with the red barn and corn crib across the road.

Few things in my life had produced such a strong sense of connection, a sense difficult to put into words. I knew the house was right for us, just as I had immediately known that Knox was the man I wanted to marry, and I have never wavered in the decision that buying it was the right thing to do, even though the children at first resisted. We sold the Goose Lane house and bought the North Guilford house in October 1971 and moved ourselves into it by Thanksgiving.

Although I had declared the place "perfect," we did make a major change, adding on a screen porch, something Knox and I, both Southerners, associated with "easy summer livin." Of course we hadn't taken into account New England's harsher climate, but the porch continued to remain the site of some of our fondest memories, of family reunions and get togethers that lasted late into the evening.

—

The house, built in 1842 as the homestead of a farmer named Christopher Columbus Rossiter, has its own life, expanding and contracting as the weather changes, creaking and sighing, shifting restlessly from time to time on its stone foundation. I love the wooden doors that can close off the rooms, providing quiet and privacy to anyone who wishes to be alone to read or write or think about something. I love the wooden floors, even those whose patches recall some long-forgotten remodeling project. I love the old imperfect windows, not only because the wavy glass subtly revises the appearance of the world outside, but because they are the very glass that made C. C. Rossiter happy that he could afford the six-over-six sashes that would flood his house with light.

In its floors and windows, its anachronistic heating and plumbing systems added long after the house was completed, the house speaks of lives lived here more

Our house in North Guilford, 1971

than a century ago. The Rossiters and those who followed them managed without cars, electricity, central heating, or running water. They grew their own food, made their own soap, and spent their leisure hours, if they had any, without radios, telephones, television, or computers. They rose at daybreak and retired at sunset, their lives focused on survival. They worked hard, protecting their poultry and livestock from predators, mending fences, feeding and caring for their animals, planting and tending their gardens, and "putting away"—preserving and storing—their food for the winter.

Knox and Caroline on their back porch, c. 1989

They ate, slept, made love, gave birth to their babies, built fires for warmth, and cared for their little ones in rooms that are now ours. Our dining room was originally the kitchen; the old cooking fireplace is covered over, but the mantel and the door to the original bake oven remain. I can picture the first Mrs. Rossiter preparing a meal, her bread coming out of the oven just in time for everyone to sit down to dinner, the room lighted by an oil lamp set in the middle of the table. Her death in childbirth five years after she moved into the house as a young bride still saddens me, especially when I walk through the former birthing-room next to our living room, once warmed by a large stove.

I came to love the property, the fields, the trees, the views out every window. I enjoy lazy summer afternoons sitting on the front porch, imagining how it would have been watching the neighbors riding by in their buggies before the road was paved. I still love this house as I continue to share its life after more than 45 years.

CHAPTER 12
NORTH GUILFORD

We moved to North Guilford in the fall of 1971. My dream had become reality; we were living in an old house in beautiful Guilford. I continued to be happy in my marriage to Knox, who had by now received tenure at Yale, for which we were thankful since it meant we would not have to move again. My connection with the art world was strengthening; my children were growing up, vigorous and healthy. What more could I ask?

After working with Madeleine Sharrer for two more years, I decided to start my own studio in our living room, which sat empty five hours a day until the children returned from school. Artist friends and I rolled up the rug, set out our easels, and began a figure-drawing class, sharing the cost of hiring models. The class went on for four years, giving me a solid following of six artists, and I began teaching other groups and getting commissions for portraits. While I was pleased about all the work, I did not want to spend the rest of my life with a make-do arrangement in the living room.

Knox and I decided that I could transform the carriage shed into a studio, but with college tuitions looming in the near future, I had to take out a construction mortgage. I paid it off in 15 years, painting portraits, giving workshops, and teaching classes, including one for teens applying to art school who needed experience working from a live model. The studio, completed in 1978, gave me a sense of empowerment; I had a room of my own and an atelier with a following, although my studio

Caroline working in the living room, 1976

Taking down the carriage shed to build the new studio

Studio finished, 1978

was collaborative, not teacher-directed like Madeleine Sharrer's.

As my fellow artists and I worked together, the group became more than an economic convenience. In 1980 we showed work in nearby Branford, an exhibit interesting for the different renderings of the same models by ten different artists. We experimented with various ways of making art, using a variety of materials and techniques, emphasizing the formal aspects of painting rather than trying to express realistically what we saw. To indulge our interest in contemporary art, we visited galleries in New York's SoHo, at the time the city's cutting-edge art neighborhood. In the years that followed, we approached the idea of collaborating more deeply.

The children, now growing into their teens, were finding and pursuing their own interests. Knox Jr., who was musically talented, attended an alternative high school and would major in music in college. Janet played the viola da gamba and the violin, at which she became accomplished, but went to Smith College, declared a pre-med major, and eventually received her MD degree from the University of Texas Medical School at San Antonio. Although Cara had taken lessons in flute, trombone, piano, and voice (her God-given best instrument), she chose to study art at Pratt Institute in Brooklyn and later received an MSW from New York University. Margi took her cello and her bicycle to the University of California in San Diego, where she became a communications major, and then received a law degree from Tulane University in New Orleans.

Peter, 14 x 24 inches, 1977

Caroline working from a model in the new studio, 1978

Panchita, 40 x 31 inches, 1977

Retia, 40 x 31 inches, 1977

Knox's career flourished. He set up his own lab to continue work on frog muscle, studying the electrical properties of muscle membranes. With post-doctoral fellows Martin Schneider and Bob Rakowski, he discovered small currents associated with the regulation of calcium release during contraction of the muscle. Later with post-docs Steve Baylor and others, he used optical indicators to study changes in calcium activity. I was proud of him and his work, and it was great to see him happy with what he and his collaborators had accomplished. Scientific meetings took him around the world: to Iran, shortly before the toppling of the shah; to Japan and Hong Kong where he visited the parents of a former lab member; and to Thailand where he trekked 40 miles. I felt good about his opportunities to travel and in fact I enjoyed staying alone in our house, painting in my studio.

⏝

Everything was not smooth sailing, however. My beloved dad died suddenly of a heart attack in the summer of 1972, a shock since he was only 67 years old. He had recently retired from his job as health commissioner of Kentucky and had moved with "his lovely Louise" into a modest ranch-style house in Frankfort. After his death, mother moved into an apartment in Lexington, a good move we thought since she was afraid to be alone in the house and, in the apartment, would be near her twin sister May and her niece. I believed Mother would be all right there—if

Knox in his lab at Yale, c. 1980

she could control her drinking—but I didn't know she had added Valium to the mix. Dad had left their physician instructions that if anything happened to him, the doctor should take care of Louise, adding that "she needed a little something."

Knox's mother, now in her 70s, came for a week every other Christmas, still bringing thoughtful and appropriate gifts, baking cookies for the children and "Texas Chewies" for Knox. She took the children on road trips out West, first Knox Jr. and Janet, and later Cara and Margi. I continued to admire her coping abilities, but our relationship had not warmed. She followed me from room to room, as she had in the past, watching me and repeating stories about people she disliked. Her list was long: people on welfare, people who took handouts, people who were fiscally irresponsible, people who could not cope, and—this was the reason behind many of those failures—people who were lazy. Among the worst offenders were the "little whipper-snappers" in her office, younger social workers who had "all those new ideas." Every year new rifts opened between Margaret and her relatives: her mother, mother-in-law, sisters, sisters-in-law, aunts and cousins. She shared her negative thoughts about Colston's wife Seeley, who continued seeing a psychiatrist and had decided to become one herself. And recently Margaret had fallen out with Knox's aunt, Janet Embry, to whom she had once been close, or so I thought: when Margaret was 13, she had lived with Aunt Janet who had wanted to adopt her. The dispute involved money.

And although Knox still tried to convince me that his mother loved me, something told me that it was not so. I could not get through to her on any emotional level; and her total lack of interest in my art suggested that she thought I belonged in the "lazy" category.

Margaret's presence always reminded me of the Secret, but I could never find the right moment to share my knowledge with Knox or figure out how to start the conversation, though my silence kept me from being totally honest with him. While I still thought that he might react emotionally to the news, I no longer believed that he would have a breakdown. And I realized that knowing the truth would open up avenues of understanding between us, particularly about his mother.

Then in the mid 1970s, when her husband was on sabbatical at Yale, Trudy Enders Huntington came to visit us in Guilford. She had a double connection with Knox. First, her father, Bob Enders, had worked under W.K. in the OSS and after W.K.'s death had taken over his job as chief instructor of the secret intelligence training school. Second, during World War II, Trudy had come to know Knox's Cambridge mentor, Richard Adrian, because Richard and his sister, as teenagers had been sent to live with the Enders family to escape the bombing raids in England.

Trudy's visit started me on a thirty-year journey that took me into uncharted territory. When Trudy mentioned her father, Knox showed mild interest, but I quickly seized on the conversation as an opening into W.K.'s past.

"Yes, but Knox's father didn't seem a good candidate for the OSS. He was a minister's son, not the sort of person who might be a spy."

"They all were minister's sons," Trudy responded.

I was unsure exactly what she meant, but perhaps she was thinking about loyalty to God and country.

Trudy suggested to Knox that he visit her father in Swarthmore, adding that Bob Enders, now retired, would certainly enjoy meeting Knox.

Knox listened politely, but when Trudy left, he dismissed the idea. Trudy's invitation, however, jolted my own curiosity about Knox's father, which dated back to the beginning of my relationship with Knox. I wanted to know about W. K. Chandler as a man, his relationship with his wife and sons, and his work at the intelligence training school. If anyone knew the details surrounding the murder-suicide, it would be Bob Enders, and a visit to him seemed an excellent opportunity to learn more, but Knox refused to consider it.

— ⌣ —

Knox was still working too hard to spend much time with our teenagers, and since his father had died when he was ten, he had no role model to follow during our children's adolescence. Knox Jr. in particular seemed to want and need a father, someone who would go fishing or play ball with him, or listen to his ideas about life. Knox did encourage his son's love for music, taking him to New York to buy guitars and traveling around to colleges that interested him. But when I periodically reminded Knox of his paternal role advising Knox Jr. about sex, he would nod as if it was a good idea, but he never managed to approach the subject. As a teenager Knox had been given free rein, probably without much parental advice, but Brownwood, Texas, was a dry town whose culture reflected its fundamentalist religion. Guilford was different. Knox Jr. spent a lot of time with his friends, and, along with his passion for music, he developed a passion for drugs, a passion that Knox Jr. kept hidden from us.

Boiling off with neighbors in North Guilford, c. 1975

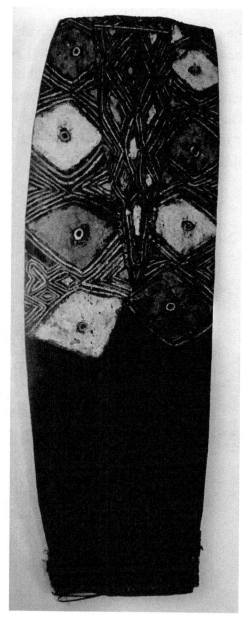

Papua New Guinea wooden shield painted with clay

CHAPTER 13
PAPUA NEW GUINEA

In 1983, with all the children out of the house, we decided to mark our 25th wedding anniversary with a trip to Australia, where the meetings of the International Physiological Society were being held. Knox, aware of my fascination with primitive art, had discovered that the natives of Papua New Guinea (PNG) still produced carvings that expressed their unspoiled cultural traditions, and he thought that we could take a side trip there.

We left on the first of July and, after stops in Hawaii, Fiji, New Zealand, and Sydney, where Knox would later attend the meetings, we flew to PNG. Our first night in Port Moresby we lay awake listening to shouting and scuffling outside our hotel window. The next morning hotel personnel informed us that the disturbance was nothing threatening, only some liquored-up local men trying to cut each other with knives. Without waiting for breakfast, we moved to the Salvation Army's protected compound and stayed there for the rest of our time in Moresby.

We first headed for the Upper Sepik River, recommended to us by Jared Diamond, a former colleague of Knox's and an expert on New Guinean bird life. For the week's trip we purchased a rolled-up foam mattress and a mosquito net; we filled one small backpack with medical supplies and toiletries and another with a stash of kinas (local coins) and a change of clothes, which we would wash in the river. As it turned out, the water stained the fabric and we took home suitcases full of deep brown clothing.

There were no roads between towns, so on July 26, a two-propeller plane deposited us at Ambunti, our starting point some 470 miles from Port Moresby. At the lodge we inquired about a guide to take us upriver and by evening three had appeared, vying for the job. We chose Kowspi, who had worked on tour boats and had the best English of the three. The next day he took us to the village of Yagi where the natives welcomed us, and Kowspi impressed Knox by rubbing sticks together to make a fire, making us doubly sure of the wisdom of our choice.

I was apprehensive about setting out for a week with someone we barely knew, so I convinced Knox that we should make an overnight trip first to make sure that we could trust Kowspi with our lives. The next day he and his cousin Benedict took us in a dugout canoe to Kowspi's village, Waskuk, where we met some of his family, shared a meal, and spent the night. We returned to Ambunti, pleased that trust had been established.

The next morning we walked a half mile to Malu, whose inhabitants spoke a language different from Ambunti, not surprising because the villages are so isolated from one another that more than 750 languages are spoken in PNG. I had brought a hand-held tape recorder and asked some of the women and children in Malu to record a song. When I played it back, their faces lit up, and as if to thank me a boy scampered up a palm tree and threw down a couple of coconuts. With a machete another boy skillfully hacked them open and handed one to each of us. The local people, whose friendly and hospitable nature impressed us, watched for our reaction as we drank the coconut milk, just as we had observed them as they listened to themselves on the recorder. We played the tape back at the lodge in Ambunti, and by the language being spoken, a young man identified the site of the recording as Malu, the village where his mother lived. The night before we were to start out, Kowspi showed Knox a map of the places he would take us: Ganga, Serenapi, and Paru on Lake Paru. Knox looked at the map of the lake and said, "Okay, but I don't see a mark for the village of Paru."

"I know, but the village is here," Kowspi replied, pointing to a spot on the edge of the lake.

"But, Kowspi," said Knox in disbelief, "how will we know when we are there." Kowspi straightened to his full stature and answered, "You will know because I will tell you."

The two men went shopping for the week's provisions, returning with a large bag of rice, tins of Spam in case we couldn't find fish or fowl, bullets for shooting the fowl in case we could find them, and gasoline for the outboard motor. Kowspi said he would need two "bullets," by which he meant shotgun shells, to shoot "two Goura pigeons." Since Knox didn't think anyone could get two birds with only two shells, he bought six.

Travel was definitely not comfortable. The canoe, carved from a single tree trunk, had neither cushions nor a canopy to shelter us from the sun. The mosquitoes, which the natives had warned were "the size of horses," attacked us ferociously at sundown. The meals, simple and repetitive, often consisted of Spam and rice. On the other hand, the people impressed us with their kindness and hospitality; in one village a family vacated its own bush house for us to stay the night. By our second day on the river Knox, sweating profusely, informed Kowspi that if PNG had air conditioning and cold beer, it would be a tourist's delight. In spite of the discomforts, we were game for whatever adventures this remarkable country had to offer us.

In Serenapi, Kowspi borrowed a gun and announced that the next morning he would go pigeon hunting. Sure enough, two shots accompanied by the chanting of the villagers awakened us. We looked out from beneath our mosquito net to see Kowspi carrying two turkey-sized birds by the feet, their crests of lacy blue feathers dragging on the ground. Later we discovered that Goura pigeons, also called Victoria crested pigeons, were endangered, but by then Kowspi's birds had already been served to us for dinner. They turned out to be "some tough birds," even after being boiled, and we dined mostly on rice that night. We never knew what happened to the other four shotgun shells, though we learned that Kowspi could sell Goura pigeon feathers in the Highlands for many kinas.

I was not prepared emotionally for our arrival at Paru. As we entered the lake in late afternoon, mist was rising from the waters, and the familiar hushed sounds evoked memories of lakes that I had visited with my father in Kentucky. He had loved taking my brother and me out in his motor boat before dawn. "Best time for a good catch," he would say, but it was the magic of the early morning with the haze floating off the lake and the sounds of the new day that I remembered from my childhood with him, so far away and so long ago. At that moment in Paru I recalled his love of nature, of streams and lakes, and how he shared that with his family. I did not fight the tears.

Every village had artisans who were occupied making masks, spirit objects, drums, shields, and arrows, all of which had significance in the native culture or religion. Because we were made to feel that we should buy something in every village we visited, we purchased dozens of carvings, and as our eyes became more experienced we could spot the difference between "authentic" works, made with the ceremonial spirit, and "airport art" sold to deplaning tourists. The "airport" carvings did not lack craftsmanship, but had been made solely to sell and in my mind lacked soul.

People would be waiting for our arrival. At one settlement on the Upper Sepik about a dozen men, each grasping long, beautifully carved arrows, stood around the house where we were to sleep. It was late and we hadn't eaten, so Kowspi suggested that we wait until morning to make our purchases, because the process would take a while. The price of the first arrow had to be negotiated and, once settled, became the price for each additional one. We were required to buy one arrow from each man before we could buy a second one from anyone. We bought a couple of dozen at one kina—the equivalent of $1.20—apiece.

While the men created carvings, the women crafted bags called bilums, making string from plant materials by rubbing the fiber on their thighs, then looping the string with their fingers, rather like crocheting. Each bag took weeks to make, and all were for sale. I learned later that the spirits of the people were interwoven with those threads, and that the bags became tokens of love, symbols of cultural difference, and markers of social standing as well as containers for spirits and magic.

I had practiced pidgin English, the language of trade. As we traveled upriver my limited language skills became useful purchasing bilums.

I would open with, "Yu gat bilum?"

The woman would answer "yesa" and I'd reply, "Aumas (how much)?"

She would come back with "Nambawan pei (number one price)" and I'd ask for the "nambatu pei." I didn't really care if she would take less, but had been told that this was the accepted way of arriving at an agreeable price. If she would not come down she would respond, "Nogat nambatu pei," or if she was willing to settle for less she would give me a second price. I came home with about one of every size bilum ever made in New Guinea including one highly prized "nambawan pei" bilum, which Kowspi explained was especially valuable because of the piece of red plastic attached to the front. With the bilum handles looped over their heads, the women carried food, firewood, and even very large loads. In one village we met a woman carrying her husband to the hospital in an oversized bilum. Later, feeling a little too sure of my pidgin English, I admired a baby boy carried by his mother in a bilum. I said "Mi laikim pikinini man," which I thought meant "I like your baby boy." The mother turned away and fled, thinking that I wanted to buy the baby, not that I thought that he was cute.

During the next leg of the journey in the Southern Highlands, we traveled from village to village in a four-wheel-drive vehicle. Although we had heard rumors that some of the tribes in the Highlands were warring, the guide assured us that we were safe. But he added that if a driver hit and killed a pig in a village, he should drive straight to the next village and ask to be jailed because "payback" would be expected, a life for a life. Although such stories may suggest that the natives are savages, they are not. Their friendly and gentle nature is captivating.

Every day there was something to do and see: we visited village markets, displaying foods and crafts that included necklaces made from shells or other natural materials, as well as wood carvings, and clay pots. We were welcomed at the "sing sings," festivals with large pots of food cooking on the sidelines and groups of villagers, arms linked, dancing and singing to drum beats, their bodies decorated with colored clay, beads, and feathers, some of them from Goura pigeons. Their desire to beautify their appearance reminded me of Madeleine Sharrer, who was very aware of the significance of clothing and the importance of colors and textures, and who had urged me to buy something beautiful to wear.

On the third part of our trip, again traveling by dugout canoe, we met up with Alan Grinnell, a physiologist from UCLA, and visited the Middle Sepik, led by a new guide, Sava. When we arrived at a village, we would be taken immediately to the "man house," a ceremonial building where the secret rituals of their animistic religion took place. Although native women were excluded, my status as a tourist permitted me to enter a space that would normally have been forbidden because of my gender. The artifacts inside, many with spiritual significance, mesmerized me; some had been made by ancestors and passed down through the generations; others seemed like found objects. There were small carvings of human figures, some with skulls instead of heads, feathers of Cassowary birds, and images from the natural world—crocodiles and even bugs—recognizable but also somewhat abstract. These artifacts had been placed on structures that looked like altars; some had been tucked away in secret corners, and their arrangement reminded me of the placement of icons within a Christian cathedral.

Some villages had a church as well as a "man house," and Christianity, introduced by missionaries, existed side by side with the native religion, a coexistence that may have distressed the Christians, but was not problematic for the New Guineans.

During our five and a half weeks in PNG, we accumulated a great many artifacts, which Sava crated for us and sent to Guilford. We returned to Australia for the meetings and the last leg of our journey. Before leaving Sydney, we celebrated our twenty-fifth anniversary by renewing our marital vows. Because I had not worn a wedding ring for years, not since my fingers had outgrown the original one, Knox bought a nine-carat gold band and slipped it on my finger as we expressed our desire to grow old together. I look back on that simple ceremony as a beautiful and tender, 18- or 24-carat moment.

The journey changed our lives for the better. We admired the New Guineans who lived simply with nature, without the possessions that we in the States think so necessary; we admired their ingenuity, which made their survival possible, their friendly and generous nature, and their integrity, which allowed us to put our lives in their hands, especially during the long canoe trip into the Upper Sepik.

Their art, particularly the sculpture, has had a lasting impact on my own work. The carved and painted wooden shield (see page 162) that has hung in our living room for more than thirty years was created to ward off evil spirits as well as hostile arrows, and remains a source of inspiration for me. It is an object in itself instead of a representation of something else, and its spiritual power is, I believe, the source of its artistic power.

The trip was an important uniting factor in our marriage. We settled back into our house in North

Guilford, and although life was forever different with all the children gone, we were thankful for all that was good in our lives and we looked forward to our future together.

Caroline with bilum crossing over a rope bridge, 1983

PART 3

What is essential is invisible to the eye.
Antoine de Saint-Exupéry, *The Little Prince* (1943)

CHAPTER 14

THE SECRET REVEALED

Sunburned, rested, and still on an adrenalin high from the excitement of our travels, Knox and I unpacked and spent hours recounting the experiences of the past two and a half months to anyone who would listen. We organized a slide show for the Physiology Department at Yale and one for our neighbors, though I don't think we successfully conveyed our enthusiasm. I imagined our audiences wondering how we could have enjoyed spending weeks outdoors in suffocating heat without the benefit of modern plumbing or celebrating our 25th anniversary in a dugout canoe on a muddy river.

We continued in our euphoric state for several weeks, until we received a phone call from my cousin in Lexington. My mother had taken a turn for the worse. Her drinking had gotten out of hand, and the manager of her apartment house had had to break into her apartment when she had passed out on the sofa leaving food burning on the stove.

We discovered that her doctor had indeed given her "a little something," Valium and something else, whose effects she enhanced with wine, which as far as she was concerned was not really alcohol, not like bourbon. She thought that she had her life in order and, perhaps for a while she did. She had been enjoying her friends and relatives, meeting them for lunch and shopping excursions, but somewhere along the way, she had lost control, and the old demon had taken over. The manager rightly feared she was a threat to the rest of his tenants. I won the coin-toss to take her from her apartment and bring her back to Connecticut.

When I told her that she needed to be near Rusty or me, her defenses went up as I expected they would. She refused to admit that she could not continue living alone and turned on me, which I also expected, dragging up the familiar litany of accusations: I was an ungrateful daughter, I wasn't as smart as I thought I was, I didn't treat her with the respect she was due, and so on. I tried to reason with her, but only when I mentioned my concerns about Rusty who had his own family problems, did she give in and agree to join me on a flight back to Connecticut.

Back home, I soon found out that taking care of mother left me no time for art. Knox was certain that we could work it out, but after two weeks she solved the problem herself. She did not want to stay in Connecticut. Period. She didn't like my cooking (I did not boil the string beans for six hours with ham hock, for example). Our house was old and cold and didn't have proper locks on the windows and doors. And so on. Although she claimed that she wanted to live with Rusty because his lifestyle was more like hers, I knew that she simply did not want to live with me when she could live with her favorite child. I was relieved for myself, but sad for Rusty. Two weeks later he arrived and took her home with him to Bradford, Pennsylvania. Our lives returned to normal and I returned to my studio.

Over the past year, my thoughts had often returned to Trudy Enders' visit. I kept trying to understand why Knox had no interest in talking to Bob Enders, though I realized that my knowledge of the Secret heightened my own urgency. Then, in the spring of 1984, Richard Adrian and his wife Lucy came from England to visit us. Richard mentioned that he and Lucy had visited Bob Enders before coming to our house.

Was he the Bob Enders who had been in the OSS during World War II, Knox wondered.

"Yes," answered Richard. "Why do you ask?"

"Well, he was under my father at the 'Farm' in Clinton, Maryland. My father was chief instructor there." As if to anticipate the next question, Knox continued, "My father committed suicide. He'd had a head injury in a car accident."

"My God, Knox, when?"

"It was 1943, July 12, when he died. I was nine and my brother was four. Bob Enders sent us to live with his family so that my mother could take care of things in Clinton."

Richard's face lit up, an unusual display of animation for him. He certainly remembered his wartime stay in Swarthmore with the Enders family, during the London bombings, and he even vaguely recalled there being smaller children visiting at the time.

"How odd that our paths crossed so long ago,"

he said. "You should go to Swarthmore to visit Bob. I am certain he would be pleased to see you."

"Yes, yes, that would be a good idea," said Knox. Then the conversation moved elsewhere.

After Richard left, I reopened the subject.

"I can't believe that with all the time you and Richard worked together in England and here at Yale, the subject of your father never came up."

"Well it didn't. When we were doing experiments, we didn't talk about other things."

Knox seemed defensive, but I pushed on anyhow. "What about going to see Dr. Enders? Richard thought it would be a good idea."

"No, I don't think so," Knox said. "I don't want to do that."

I couldn't believe that he had told Richard that a visit would be a good idea, but now he said he had no intention of going. I took a deep breath. "I think you should go to visit Dr. Enders."

I could see the physical resistance in his body. "I don't want to do that," he repeated.

I persevered. "Dr. Enders is an old man and might not live much longer. Maybe he could tell you more about your father."

Knox started to get up as if the conversation was over. "I doubt if he could tell me anything that I don't already know. Why are you acting this way?"

That did it, the "why."

"Sit down," I said, "and I will tell you why." My legs

started shaking, so I sat down, too.

"There is a secret about your father's death. Your mother has kept it from you and Colston."

Though I had rehearsed telling him many times, I didn't know how he was going react. I started guardedly.

"When we were in Brownwood for Knox Jr.'s baptism, I said to Aunt Meggs that I'd never seen a photo of your father and she brought out an album full of family photographs."

Knox looked at me blankly. "While I was looking at the pictures, a newspaper clipping fell out. It had an article about your father's death. It said he shot himself after fatally wounding a woman he worked with."

There, I had actually said it. I had imagined this moment for years and now I had actually told Knox the Secret. I was still shaking as I watched to see how the news affected him. He had no visible reaction whatsoever, absolutely none. I had worried for 26 years that the news might overwhelm him, but he seemed to have no emotional connection to his father. I had anticipated that he would be interested in visiting Dr. Enders after hearing about the murder, but he still seemed indifferent.

His only response was, "What paper was the article in? I'd like to get hold of a copy."

"It was the *Chicago Sun*. You know, it was so long ago that I am beginning to wonder if I read it correctly... but how could I have imagined a murder."

When Knox produced a copy from the Yale Library, the article said exactly what I recalled, and after reading it, Knox agreed to go to Swarthmore if I would make the arrangements. I still thought his reluctance strange, but I wrote to Dr. Enders introducing Knox and me, and mentioning the connection with Richard Adrian. Enders answered that a visit would be fine, but not until October.

In August 1984, we threw an 80th birthday celebration for Knox's mother, since Margaret refused to have a party in Brownwood, saying that she would not know how to draw the line on whom to invite. Colston and Seeley were on sabbatical in Chicago, so we took on the party by default. The gathering consisted of Margaret, our family of six and the five Colston Chandlers.

We went all out, arranging a lobster dinner, gifts, and champagne toasts. I was startled when Margaret commented afterwards that what she really liked was steak, so we cooked a second celebratory meal. After all the wining and dining and the departure of the Colston Chandlers, Knox and I took Margaret on a whirlwind tour of Martha's Vineyard to visit her cousin and a driving trip around Massachusetts and southern Vermont. She enjoyed the sights and also the attention, sitting in the front passenger seat next to Knox so that he could point out the scenery to her.

We planned to tell her what we had learned about Knox's father's death before she left for Texas, thinking that she would be relieved that she wouldn't have to keep the Secret any longer, that we could have a heart-to-heart talk about Knox's father. We also thought that she might be interested in knowing that we planned to visit Dr. Enders.

We could not have been more wrong.

After dinner the day before she was to leave. Knox started, "Caroline and I want to tell you that we know the truth about what happened when my father killed himself. Caroline has known for a long time, but she just recently told me."

Margaret stiffened; her lips tightened, but her face became otherwise expressionless. Her silence thickened the air in the room. I could not imagine what was going on in the head of this complicated woman, but I remembered all too clearly the discomfort of our first meeting. When Margaret had confronted me all those years ago, I had been tongue-tied, but now the words tumbled out.

"I found out accidentally, when we were back in Texas for Knox Jr.'s baptism."

I waited. She didn't respond, so I went on. "The Chicago newspaper clipping fell into my lap from Aunt Meggs' photo album, the blue one." I said it slowly, drawing out the words, as if it were a question, hoping for some acknowledgment, but she made no sound, only stared straight ahead, not looking at either Knox or me. Her body remained rigid, almost catatonic.

"I read only part of the article. I was in shock. I didn't know what to do. I wanted to talk about it but I was afraid. I wanted to talk to Knox about it but I couldn't bring myself to do it. All these years I hated keeping the Secret, especially from Knox."

She seemed not to hear, but sat stonily, looking straight ahead. I went on, a little desperately. "It never seemed the right time to tell Knox, not until Richard Adrian came to visit and said that Knox should visit Bob Enders. We are going in the fall."

Knox and I sat there, looking at his mother, not saying anything. I had no idea what he was thinking. He had let me do all the talking, but after a few painful moments, he tried to get her to say something, telling her that we thought that what she had gone through was a terrible experience, that we thought that she would be relieved and would want to talk about it. She refused to acknowledge his words and if anything became more physically rigid. I could have predicted that she had no interest in my feelings about having kept the Secret for so long, but I was surprised that she did not seem to care how Knox must have felt learning the news.

Knox told her that it was better to know the truth and that Colston should also know.

That unleashed the anger she had been visibly controlling. With clenched teeth, she hissed, "I do not want you to tell Colston." She paused. The anger seemed to play itself out. With a far-away look in her eyes, she said, "I didn't think he wanted a divorce."

What a strange thing to say; her words still haunt me. She went back to Texas refusing to say another word about Knox's father, and barely speaking to us.

She had kept the Secret from Knox and Colston for 41 years; she had managed to prevent the immediate family, more distant relatives, and the Brownwood community from revealing the truth to the boys while they were growing up. To do so, she had destroyed or hidden letters, photographs, and newspaper articles except for the one clipping that Aunt Meggs had kept. And now the Secret was out. The revelation must have been devastating.

I began to wonder about Aunt Meggs. Had she forgotten to hide the clipping? Or had she deliberately placed it with other family photos? And had she remembered that it was in the Blue Album when she handed it to me? Her selection and careful preservation of photos certainly showed that she cherished her family and was close to her brother. Might she have longed for his life to be recognized, not hidden away as if he had never existed? The photographs of W. K. obsessed me—the snapshots of him as a baby, a child, a young man, and finally a married man and father with two sons. I began to see a family connection; his eyes had the same intensity of focus and underlying playfulness that I saw in my husband's. I could see the genetic connection linking the three Knox Chandlers—W. K., my husband, and my son—and I realized I wanted to know more.

CHAPTER 15
THE VISIT TO DR. ENDERS

Dr. Enders proposed October 26, 1984, as the day for us to talk about Knox's father, and he sent very detailed directions for driving to his home in Swarthmore, Pennsylvania. The house turned out to be small and quaint, a little bedraggled, with overgrown bushes leaning against the foundations and cobwebs hanging from the window frames. I had unrealistically expected to find a busy household, filled with students and guests, teenagers, and children, as it had been during World War II when Richard Adrian lived there. But in 1984, the house seemed forlorn and I reminded myself that a couple in their eighties now lived there.

Abbie Enders greeted us warmly at the door and ushered us down a long dark hall narrowed by towering stacks of musty books. Dr. Enders waited for us in the living room. He had retired as chair of Swarthmore's zoology department in 1970, and was now frail, his right hand afflicted with a conspicuous tremor. As a young man he must have been good looking and even now his height and the thick shock of white hair that stood straight up from his forehead gave him a forceful presence. Sitting upright, as if at attention, in a straight chair, he removed his watch from his wrist and placed it face up on the table in front of him. I was already apprehensive, and the formality of the setting as well as the atmosphere of the room added to my uneasiness. Abbie gestured that we should take the two chairs facing him.

Enders greeted us briefly and launched into what seemed a prepared account of W. K.'s death, lecturing as if we were undergraduates attending one of his classes. In the summer of 1943, he began, W. K. had been under enormous stress; the number of recruits coming to the training facility had more than doubled in anticipation of the D-Day invasion the following spring; there were more students and fewer instructors; the recruits would be sent behind enemy lines and many would die. W. K., finding it difficult to sleep, grew ever more jittery and distraught. He may have been further demoralized by doubts, continued Enders, unable to accept without question the dictum that the end justifies the means, which Enders himself found appropriate during wartime, but which troubled W. K. On more than one occasion Enders had found him, uncharacteristically, drinking beer during the day.

Knox spoke up. "I was told that my father had injured his head in a car accident," he suggested, implying that the crash might have contributed to W. K.'s atypical behavior.

"There was no accident," said Enders unequivocally ending discussion of the topic.

Enders went on. He had arrived at Rosemary Sidley's house shortly after the murder-suicide. Her lighted cigarette, still burning, was clenched between her fingers. The bodies were outside the house. W. K. was a good marksman (something of which Enders seemed proud) and had shot Rosemary through her wrist into her heart before turning the gun on himself and sending a bullet into his brain.

"I don't understand," I said, "the newspaper article said that the bodies were found in the house."

Enders jerked his head around to look at me in a way that suggested that he was unaccustomed to being interrupted.

He hesitated a second and then bristled. "I... I told the newspapers what to say." Not giving us a chance to interrupt again, he described W. K.'s head injury in excruciating detail, perhaps because he thought that Knox as a doctor would be interested, but his gory depiction seemed insensitive to me. He went on to talk about the reputed love affair between W. K. and Rosemary Sidley, claiming that the relationship was platonic, but then remarking that he had burned the "love letters."

After the 50-minute lecture ended, Dr. Enders called for Abbie to serve tea and the conversation switched to Knox's connection with the Adrian family. We were given no opportunity to ask any further questions.

As we drove away, a sense of absolute disbelief swept over me.

"What was that all about?" I asked. "Dr. Enders said that he found the bodies outside the house and that Rosemary's lighted cigarette was clutched in her hand. But if he told the newspapers what to say, he told them that the police had found them inside. He claimed the relationship between your father and Rosemary was platonic, but then told the newspapers that your father killed Rosemary and himself because she had rejected him as a lover. He also said that he had burned the love letters. It just doesn't make sense." I began to wonder whether he had told us the truth. Was there something Enders was keeping from us? Or had I been keeping a secret all these years that wasn't even true? My head was swimming.

Robert K. Enders, c. 1970

Knox, slow to speak, seemed equally mystified. "It certainly confuses the story," he said.

A few days later Knox wrote Enders thanking him for his hospitality, adding, "As frequently happens, the new information has allowed new questions to develop although somewhat slowly, and perhaps naturally, many of them pertain to pre-OSS years. In many ways, my father remains an enigma."

We agreed that the visit had left us with more questions than answers. We could not understand the discrepancies between what Enders had told us and what the newspapers had published, especially since he asserted that he had told the newspapers what to say. But why had he lied to the reporters? And how had he gotten to the crime scene so soon?

CHAPTER 16
THE BLOWUP AND FINAL BREAK

As Christmas approached I felt increasingly uneasy about Margaret's scheduled holiday visit. Her cold silence when we told her we knew about the murder, her explosive anger when Knox said we would tell Colston, and her stubborn refusal to talk about relationships filled me with apprehension. Clearly she was concerned only about her own feelings. I continued to find it strange that Knox was so emotionally disengaged from his father that the discovery that W. K. had killed someone barely touched him. But I was relieved that I had worried needlessly about Knox's mental health. We determined to tell Colston when he came to visit in March, even knowing that Margaret would strongly disapprove.

Shortly before Christmas we picked her up at the airport. Our daughters arrived later that day and we all enjoyed a happy family reunion. On Christmas, as we gave and received presents and ate a traditional Christmas dinner, everything went smoothly. The next day after breakfast, Margaret launched her attack.

"After... after that birthday week here," she began, not knowing exactly what to call last summer's confrontation, "I went back to Texas and removed you both from my will. And I took you off my bank account," she said looking Knox straight in the eye. "But later, because I couldn't live with it, I put you back in my will."

He was stunned, visibly hurt, and furious that she had insulted me by cutting me out of the will, though the money meant little to me. Knox pointed out that I had taken care of her when she broke her leg, invited her for many Christmases, organized a major birthday celebration, and been more than just a "good" daughter-in-law. She had also insulted him, he added, by thinking that he might steal from her checking account.

Margaret continued on the offensive.

"Well, some time ago when I said that you had never written a check on my account, Caroline said you didn't have any checks. I didn't know what you would have done if you did have some checks."

I tried to say that my remark had been a joke, but she rejected my explanation.

"Mother," Knox asked, "do you trust anyone, anyone at all?"

"Yes," she whispered, "I trust Colston." She looked at us accusingly. "I feel that you and Caroline would try to take my house away from me. Caroline took her mother away from her apartment in Louisville, and she could do that to me."

Knox explained that my mother had had too much to drink and left food burning on the stove, so that the manager had asked me and Rusty to move her out before she set the building on fire. Margaret said nothing. Maybe she thought Knox was lying.

In the silence, he asked the crucial question. Did her dislike of me and her distrust of us arise because I had revealed the truth about W. K.'s death?

"I don't want to talk about THAT," she spat out the words angrily, "and I do not want you to tell Colston."

Knox replied that he was grateful I had told him, that he thought Colston should know, and that he was going to tell him. That set her off again. She picked up the knife next to her plate and pointed it at me.

"I never did like you, not from the beginning," she hissed. "You are a husband snatcher and a gold digger." She stabbed the knife toward me in the air, harder and harder as she listed my flaws. "You are a manipulative, demanding, and controlling wife."

There was a momentary silence.

"You are dead wrong," Knox responded. "Caroline has been a wonderful wife to me and a wonderful mother to our children."

Margaret shoved her chair back from the table and stood up. "I want to go home. Tomorrow," she said. "And if you think that I am going to lose any sleep over this, you are wrong." She strode from the room.

The intensity of her hostility toward me took us by surprise. I had picked up on her lack of physical and emotional connection to others, and I had seen her willingness to cut off longstanding relationships over trivial matters, but I had naïvely hoped that I would escape the ill will she often directed at other women in the family. Back in 1959, she had broken with her sisters-in-law over Grandmother Chandler's small inheritance and had refused to talk about the misunderstanding. She had been on cool terms with her own mother and sisters for years.

Although it hurt me, I could also accept the fact that she had not liked me from our first meeting, but I could not understand why she called me a husband snatcher. Did she confuse me with Rosemary Sidley, with whom her husband was supposedly involved? Nor could I figure out why she branded me a gold digger. If I had planned to marry Knox for his prospective earnings as a doctor, surely I would have broken off the relationship when he told me that he was going into research instead.

I could also understand her reasons for pretending to like me, but her deceit still rankled. If she had expressed her hostility openly, she would have had less contact with her son and her grandchildren. If I had known that she thought me a gold digger and a manipulator, I would have found it difficult to invite her to stay with us on holidays or in England, and I certainly would have not wanted to take her into our home for several months when she broke her leg.

Knox was able to convince his mother to stay until her scheduled flight, but that night, unlike Margaret, I did lose sleep, and the next day the atmosphere was so venomous that we could barely breathe. Knox and I had hoped for a "morning after" reconciliation, but Margaret distanced herself as if she had already left.

After she returned to Texas, Knox wrote, pleading with her to talk to someone, perhaps a social worker, about her relationship with me. When she didn't respond, I wrote saying that it seemed that nothing could change her mind, that there was no hope of mending our relationship unless we could communicate on some level. Again she didn't answer, and I returned her Christmas and birthday checks.

⌣

Colston and Seeley came to visit us in March, Colston from Hungary and Seeley from Chicago. We hadn't told them about the Secret or the blowup with Margaret, thinking it more appropriate to break the news in person. Like Knox, Colston did not react visibly to the revelation that his father had killed someone.

Despite the lack of encouragement, I pushed on and told them of Margaret's accusations and her subsequent refusal to communicate. I asked Seeley whether she thought Margaret was suffering from paranoia. Aware that Margaret had always thought of her as sick because she was seeing a psychotherapist, Seeley replied that eighteen years of her mother-in-law's disapproval made it difficult to be dispassionate, but she did wonder why Margaret would pretend to like me all those years and then write me off, because I revealed the truth to Knox. Our visit ended without any real discussion of the Secret, but we promised to keep in touch. In a letter that same year, Seeley remarked that W. K.'s deed was truly horrific, "like a nuclear bomb in a way, a complete disaster in the center but affecting people at great distance, too."

⌣

Knox had begun a letter to his mother early in the year, but put it aside in anger. He finished it in April, and mailed it before she visited Colston's family. He reiterated his belief in the importance of truthfulness and expressed his unhappiness that she thought we would take financial advantage of her. He mentioned the long list of people whom she had criticized or broken with in the past, a list that now seemed to include us, and he asked why she thought we were untrustworthy, why she thought so poorly of me, and what she meant by "family is everything," a mantra she frequently repeated. He signed it, "Love, Knox."

In May, Margaret visited Colston and Seeley, who tried, fruitlessly, to intervene in my behalf. Seeley, however, did solve the "gold digger" mystery. Margaret bitterly recalled that I had returned the baptismal outfit for Knox Jr., and she mistakenly thought I had kept the money for myself, thus in her mind becoming forever selfish and greedy, a gold digger. Seeley added later in a letter that Margaret was unable to let bygones be bygones and harbored so many grievances that it was difficult to get beyond each concrete experience.

In August, Knox got a letter at work, with "PERSONAL" written in red capital letters across the envelope. (Margaret had sent it to his office, afraid that I would open it.) After six pages of chit-chat, Margaret turned to Knox's April letter:

"Some of the things you said puzzled me and, really, I do not know how to reply to it so I decided that the 'no comment' method was the best. I know now that I was too hasty in having your name removed from my bank accounts. In order to have it reinstated, I had to have new cards made—will you please sign the cards and return to me so I can send them to the bank."

She closed saying, "I still love you and you will always be my precious big boy."

Knox wrote back, incidentally asking her not to send letters to his lab:

"I am disappointed that your response was 'no comment.' Which things puzzled you? Your behavior has given me much emotional concern as I described. And I am not 'a precious big boy,' I am a grown man who would like to interact with you as a grown son. I find 'no comment' to the issues expressed as being inconsistent with motherly love. I hope that you will reconsider and discuss the points expressed in the letter. If not, then a 'no comment' relationship we shall have."

Margaret never responded, not even with another "no comment."

Margaret's manner of expressing her love for her son continued to trouble me. I had never heard her say the words "I love you" to anyone, not even to him, and she apparently found it easier to communicate affection in a backhanded way rather than directly.

Wondering about Margaret's life before I met her, I phoned several family members who had known her for many years. Aunt Meggs expressed surprise at the blowup because she thought that Margaret had already told the boys about the tragedy. Margaret had never said anything negative about me, but praised my cooking and admired the way I managed her 80th birthday party. And since Margaret had shown her love and pride in her family through the years by her actions and words, Meggs could not believe she had meant the things she had said at Christmas.

I also wrote to Margaret's younger sister, Aunt Elizabeth, whom I had never met. As far as Elizabeth knew, Margaret had never mentioned any hostility toward me. She was sure that if we continued to show our love for her, things would be all right. Margaret had told me, and Elizabeth confirmed, that as the eldest daughter she was blamed when anything went wrong. Elizabeth had been sickly; Foncie, as "the baby" on whom everyone doted, was never held responsible.

The girls' mother had tuberculosis and occasionally went away for a "cure," but even when she was home, her health prevented her from dealing with sibling conflicts, so she would threaten Margaret in the time-honored way, "You just wait until your father gets home." He would arrive, take off his belt, and whip her. With obvious pride, Margaret had told me that many years later her dad had apologized for the whippings, an apology that proved to her that "he was in the wrong and I was in the right." Elizabeth said that Margaret and her mother had quarreled over the apology and never resolved their differences.

Margaret's tale about the whippings suggests that she felt she was treated unjustly. She wanted life to be fair, but she also wanted to be seen as always right while others, by contrast, were wrong. Her difficulties relating to people were perhaps rooted in her childhood when her pattern of estrangement from family members began.

Through the years Elizabeth had come to believe that Margaret felt unloved much of her life, though no one realized it. Since Margaret felt unloved growing up, she seemed unable to express love in return, though as an adult she offered affection on her own terms performing acts of kindness that seemed calculated rather than spontaneous. But throughout her life her emotional ties remained fragile and easily broken.

When Margaret became too old to live alone, Knox went to Texas to help her move from Brownwood to a retirement home in Dallas. While he was there, he again tried to convince her that she was mistaken about me. One night, after a day spent packing, Margaret decided that they should drive 32 miles to a Mexican restaurant for dinner. On the way back, she said, rather emotionally, "I am so-o-o sorry," and Knox began to hope that his efforts at reconciliation had borne fruit, that Margaret had come to regret the family rift. But she continued, "I'm sorry that the dinner wasn't better, after we went all that way." The remark convinced him that his mother cared more about the rice and beans at a Tex-Mex restaurant than she did about her family.

⌣

I saw Margaret for the last time in 1989. Margi and I drove from California to New Orleans where she would enter Tulane Law School, and we made plans to stop in Albuquerque with Colston. After we had finalized our itinerary, I got an unexpected phone call from Margaret, asking us to visit her at her retirement home.

Since we hadn't communicated for five years, I was torn between my sense of grievance and Margi's opportunity to visit the grandmother for whom she had been named. Seeley suggested that Margaret had mellowed, and Margi did want to see her grandmother, so I agreed to stop in Dallas, even though I recognized that Seeley might be mistaken.

Margi and I set out in her ancient Datsun, which had no air conditioning and a wrench instead of a crank for the front passenger window. After what seemed an endless trip through the desert, we arrived in Albuquerque where Colston confided that he thought his mother remained as intransigent as ever. But he fixed us a nice dinner and poured us each a refreshing cold beer, which momentarily quieted my anxiety about the next day's visit.

When Margi and I pulled up in front of the retirement home, I thought that the wiser course would be to remain in the car, but trying to be courteous I tentatively followed Margi into her grandmother's cottage. Margaret folded Margi into a big hug, but as I approached, she stiffened, extended her arms, and flapped her hands at me like windshield wipers, warning me not to come closer. Stunned by this reception, I sat down on a nearby chair, took a few deep breaths, and resolved not to say anything. I had never had an anxiety attack, but I thought my first might be coming any minute. The conversation between Margi and her grandmother floated past me, but after a few minutes, I realized that Margaret was holding forth on discipline, one of her favorite topics, praising Knox for the way he had punished Knox Jr. for wrecking the family car, but mixing up the details of the story with another incident.

My good intentions evaporated. My hurt feelings still close to the surface even after five years made it impossible for me to sit silently.

"All wrong," I blurted. "All wrong. It didn't happen that way at all." I refused to listen to her concoct a story out of thin air. I knew I shouldn't have come, that nothing had changed, that she still reworked history to suit her point of view. I got up and walked out, feeling ashamed of my behavior even as I headed for the car.

As I waited, I realized that Margaret had deceived Seeley, concealing her resentment so that Margi and I would stop to see her. I determined never to let anything like that happen again. Margaret lived ten more years, but I never saw or spoke to her again. Surely, I thought, there was something wrong with this woman who manipulated others seemingly without a single pang of guilt. I turned my thoughts toward my husband and my family, and began working harder on my art and on the exciting things happening in my studio.

CHAPTER 17
FROM THE BLOWUP TO REHAB

After we confronted Margaret with our knowledge of the Secret, we hoped that our lives would become less stressful so that Knox could concentrate on his science and I could work on my art. It was not to be. Nor would I find time to satisfy my renewed curiosity about W. K., reawakened by Trudy Enders' visit. But in many ways life seemed to be proceeding happily. Knox's work was progressing. The girls had graduated from college and were pursuing their careers. Knox Jr. was in New York, arranging, composing, and performing.

But one April night in 1988, the phone woke us from a deep sleep. At that hour it could only be bad news. I fumbled in the dark for the receiver, gripped with fear. Laura, Knox Jr.'s wife, was on the line. Knox Jr. was missing and she had no idea where he was. His friends had not seen him for more than 24 hours. She had phoned all the hospitals in Manhattan and the police. She was frantic. But she promised to call back when she had some news.

We knew that our son had been struggling with drugs since high school, and that he had tried to stop using, but we now knew he had failed.

Knox looked crushed, but then he burst out, "Why does he do this to us? Why does he have to do this?" The anger in his voice only added to the pain of Laura's news.

Waiting to hear from her was almost unbearable,

but we knew she was on her phone calling anyone who might know anything, and there was little point in trying to get in touch with her. The next day when our phone finally rang, Knox answered and I picked up on the other line. Between sobs Laura told us that Knox Jr. had been dumped on their doorstep by friends early in the morning. He was not hurt, but she thought he needed to get into rehab, right away.

She and her father were looking into the possibilities. He knew of an affordable facility nearby, but it had a long waiting list. He then recommended Conifer Park near Albany, which had an opening but was expensive. Eight thousand dollars for a month of rehab, she said.

Knox swallowed hard. We just didn't have that kind of money since we were still paying off debts from Cara's and Margi's college tuitions, and Janet was planning a wedding. But Laura begged us to come down to the city. It would help Knox Jr. to see us. Maybe it would help us to see him.

Knox promised to get back to her and hung up. I met him in the living room. Still shaken and furious, he asked me what we should do.

"Let's think about it," I said. "Maybe we can borrow. But I think we should go down to the city...tonight." Knox nodded.

We dreaded confronting Knox Jr., thinking that he would be humiliated to be seen in such a desperate state, but when we arrived at their apartment in the East Village, humiliation was the least of his problems. His gaunt body and ashen appearance shocked us, but when he began to tell us of his tactile hallucinations, that bugs were coming out of his skin, we realized that Knox Jr. had hit bottom. He was 30 years old.

We turned to Laura who by now was composed and very much in charge of the situation. She said Conifer Park could send a car for him the next morning and that during the month of treatment he would go through withdrawal and rehabilitation, attend meetings, and receive counseling.

Conifer Park sounded like the best solution, so after discussing the expense we agreed to split the cost with Laura and Knox Jr. When we were ready to leave, Knox Jr. walked us down to the car and, as we said our goodbyes, asked whether we could give him some money, just a little. We gave him ten dollars. Laura told us later that he had bought drugs and was shooting up while being driven to Conifer Park the next morning.

When we arrived home, Knox Jr. phoned to tell us to be sure to bathe because the sofa where we had been sitting was infested with bugs—how sad that this talented musician, our son, had fallen so low. My heart cried out for my firstborn; he had been an adorable little boy and a cheerful, easy child. As a teenager, however, he had become secretive and begun to pull away from the family. I had wanted to talk to him about it, but I was advised to let go of the apron strings and to allow him to grow into his own person and to develop his own gifts. I was also naïve about Guilford, which I had thought idyllic, but which in fact had an active drug scene.

From childhood Knox Jr.'s only interest had been music. When he was applying to college Knox had taken him to see most of the outstanding schools and conservatories in the Northeast: the Berklee School of Music and the New England Conservatory in Boston, the University of Massachusetts and Hampshire College, Juilliard in New York, and Bard College about 90 miles north of the city. He chose Bard, where he maintained his longstanding interest in the guitar, but was also drawn to classical composition and free jazz. As a music major he was required to play an orchestral instrument so he took up the acoustic bass and before long was good enough to play in the college orchestra. His improvisatory talents were evident even then. Not content with playing the notes on the page, he could draw a remarkable palette of sounds from the bass. We saw him perform in New York as the solo accompanist for a dance troupe, about which the *New York Times* reviewer remarked that "the musician was very good and deserved a better dance group." He graduated with honors and seemed headed for a satisfying career.

But as his reputation as a rock musician developed and he began playing gigs from Boston to New York, Knox Jr. became lost in the drug world. Looking back, we were clueless for too long, and he did a good job hiding the severity of his illness. He had tried to go cold turkey several times but never succeeded. He had gone to a psychiatrist who had told him that there was no need to go the "cultish" route of Narcotics Anonymous. His music was suffering, although he thought he was playing well. Laura was also using drugs and the two got more and more deeply involved until Knox Jr. hit bottom. In retrospect, it was fortunate. It was also fortunate that he got into rehab at Conifer Park.

Knox and I spent hours going over and over the details of Knox Jr.'s life. I dissolved into tears, while Knox continued to express anger. After a week of this we agreed that we needed help. Although I was frightened and didn't know where to turn, I was determined not to keep our son's addiction secret. A neighbor who had gone through a similar ordeal with her daughter advised us, for our own sake, to get to a Narcotics Anonymous meeting right away.

The following Saturday night Knox and I set out for the Nar-Anon group in New Haven. Knox drove. While I was reading to myself a letter that had arrived from Conifer Park, Knox bitterly commented, "This is some way for us to spend a Saturday night!" I cringed at his tone of voice.

The letter contained an invitation to a family weekend at the rehab center, and included a list of places to stay. I immediately said I wanted to accept, to go see Knox Jr.

Without hesitating for a second Knox said, "Well, I'm not going."

I was horrified. I asked whether he had become completely indifferent to his son's future, but he kept on driving in stony silence.

"Well, I'm going," I said finally, "even if I have to go alone." We did not talk the rest of the way.

Downstairs in the church, the young man in charge welcomed us and explained that we were to introduce ourselves and tell why we had come. When my turn came, I was so overcome with tears that I could not say anything. Knox told our story and said that our son was in rehab at Conifer Park. After everyone had spoken, we all said the Lord's Prayer and were told to keep attending the meetings. As the group broke for coffee and cookies, a man approached Knox and gave him a big hug and said that his wife had been at Conifer Park, that it was a wonderful place, and that if we got an opportunity to go to the family weekend, we absolutely should do it. Then we all thanked the organizers who had run the session and the volunteers who had prepared the refreshments, and we left.

It was ten o'clock, and I already knew that attending a Nar-Anon meeting was not Knox's idea of a pleasant evening, but as we got back onto I-95, he began talking.

"I don't know what happened, but when that man came up and gave me a hug after the meeting, and said we should go to the family weekend... it was as if a load was lifted off my shoulders. I felt much better."

This expression of emotion was unlike Knox.

"I'll go," he said. "We should go. I don't know what I was thinking earlier."

Knox's sudden release of his anger was inexplicable to both of us at the time, but later we realized that perhaps it was the power of the group's non-judgmental acceptance, their genuine concern for his well-being and their offering of hope that sparked his change of heart. Knox did not seem to mind that the next Nar-Anon meeting also took place on Saturday night. I managed to get out a few words without falling apart, and he talked easily, as if pleased to be sharing his thoughts.

We arrived at the wooded campus of Conifer Park the next weekend. Tulips and daffodils bordered the walkways leading to the modern main building, whose large plate-glass windows seemed open and welcoming. Staff members explained the protocol of the visit, and then we met Knox Jr., who looked a great deal better than when we had last seen him.

The visiting families were told that addiction is a disease to which some people are more susceptible than others. We learned about dealing with our addicted loved ones, getting off what the program calls the merry-go-round of addiction: the addict on the merry-go-round, chasing after the drug of choice; his family also on the merry-go-round, chasing after the addict. We were counseled to take care of ourselves physically and emotionally, attend Nar-Anon meetings, and work the Twelve Steps, developed by Alcoholics Anonymous and adopted by Nar-Anon as the road to recovery. In a session directed by a counselor, we sat across from our son and spoke honestly to one another about our feelings. The two Knoxes did most of the talking, expressing their love for each other, which I found heart-warming even in the midst of our pain.

The day exhausted us. We went back to our motel and watched the TV until we fell asleep. Sunday we attended more meetings and had the opportunity to ask questions. Knox wondered about Knox Jr.'s chances for recovery. When the staff refused to answer the question, we assumed that the statistics were not good.

⌣

We began attending the Al-Anon meetings in Guilford because there was no local Nar-Anon group. My own journey included recovery from a broken ankle that I had suffered earlier in the year falling on the ice behind our house, not surprising since people dealing with a loved one's addiction are often worried, preoccupied, and accident-prone.

Although Knox was planning to go to Japan at the end of April, I could not see my way to join him, especially because Knox Jr. would get out of rehab the day he was scheduled to leave. But in the meetings, people told me that I that I should go, that I had to detach, that it was Knox Jr.'s job to stay clean, not mine, and that I was supposed to take care of myself. So with my leg still in a cast, Knox and I left for a three-week trip to Japan.

Knox Jr. left rehab at the end of April and returned to the city, back to the music world, and back to Laura who was still using drugs. What were his chances of staying clean? A psychologist in New Haven had warned us not to get our hopes up, that this rehab might be the first of many.

We returned from Japan and to the Nar-Anon meetings, which gave us strength to carry on, to get off the merry-go-round. Knox Jr. was still clean in August, and with financial help from Laura's mother, he and Laura went to Vermont for the month, where, encouraged by Knox Jr., Laura was able to get off the drugs. At the month's end, they returned to New York.

With each passing week, we became more hopeful. Knox and I could talk more freely about our role in the family problems. We believed that by concentrating on ourselves and our own short- comings, by continuing to attend meetings, we might close the distance between us and our son. Gradually we were able to rebuild the trust we had lost. Two years later, we learned from the staff at Conifer Park that Knox Jr. was the only one of his group who was still clean.

Ultimately our family benefitted from those difficult years. Cara realized that she was susceptible to alcohol addiction and began her own recovery. I benefitted from the healing power of the Twelve-Step program and felt sad for people, like my mother, who could never take the first step. I believe that the steps can be healing for other family dysfunctions—they were for us.

CHAPTER 18
THE OTHER'S ARM

During the decade from the mid-1970s to the mid-80s, I felt both a rising confidence and a deepening pleasure in my art. In particular, our trip to Papua New Guinea inspired me to explore new directions and new materials. Our involvement with Knox Jr., coping with his addiction, was certainly a distraction, and I was anxious to get back to my studio.

But just as I began to feel optimistic about Knox Jr.'s future, my artistic life suffered a major blow. I had been working in my studio with eight other women for longer than a decade, and while we had originally banded together to share the cost of models, over the years we had bonded socially, enjoying each other's company outside the studio. More important, we had bonded intellectually. We read and discussed books and reviews, attended artists' talks, and checked out the offerings of galleries, locally and in New York; we talked about art constantly. As our relationship deepened, we started searching for new directions in our work and about collaborating artistically. We had concluded as a group that a creative work of art is a dialogue between the artist and the material at hand, and we thought it might not be too much of a stretch for us to work together not only verbally but artistically, to create a dialogue between nine women and the material. We just had to figure out how to proceed.

After lengthy consideration, we chose collage as the medium. Each artist would start a collage at home and bring it the following week for discussion. We would draw numbers from a hat and take home someone else's collage to work on for the next meeting. The only rule was that the artist must have a dialogue with the piece she took home, respond to it in a way that respected the original work, just as a verbal conversation respects the words of the other speaker. She could paint over, pull off, paste on, or adjust the work in any way she wanted, but she must be able to defend her changes, to show that a dialogue with the work had truly directed her process. We worked like this until

"Intra-Facia," by the Collaborative, 48 x 70 inches, 1988

we unanimously deemed the work finished, which could take several weeks or even a year.

For want of a better name we called ourselves "Etcetera" and continued our experiment until 1986 when we felt ready to show a body of completed work. Our show in the large gallery space of the Guilford Art Center drew positive comments. Encouraged by the feedback and our own sense of accomplishment, we now felt ready to go forward with our collaboration as a viable process, not just an experiment.

My studio had become too small, so we rented a bigger space, and began working on large easel-mounted canvases. The dialogue rule remained in force. Two artists painted for a while, then two others took over. The energy that came out of this process amazed us all; no single person directed, and the work developed like an improvisational dance or musical performance. Christine Ingraham, then curator of the Madison Gallery in the next town, offered us a show in 1988, "A Woman's Show/A Dialogue. " While we had previously organized our own shows, this was our first invitational exhibition, a big step forward we thought. Most of the work was collaborative, but some of us also exhibited individual pieces.

Inevitably the collaborative work brought about changes and inspired confidence in our individual work. I began feeling a new freedom to experiment. In college I had been moved by van Gogh and Gauguin, because they had relinquished the idea that a painting had to represent something realistically. Later I had found inspiration

A Woman's Show/A Dialogue

oil/collage – collaborative

The collaborative and individual
works of nine women artists

Collaborative Work

1.	I am a wall, 1986–87, mixed media on wood panel	$4200
2.	Intra-Fascia, 1987, mixed media on hexacomb	3800
3.	Two Square, 1986–87, mixed media on hexacomb	2500
4.	Square Too, 1986–87, mixed media on hexacomb	2500
	3 & 4 (as a pair)	4500
5.	Trope I, 1986–87, oil on hexacomb	2000
6.	Trope II, 1986–87, oil on hexacomb	2000
	5 & 6 (as a pair)	3500
7.	Luna, 1987, mixed media on wood panel	2000
8.	Subjunction, 1987, mixed media on wood panel	2800
9.	Umbra, 1987, mixed media on wood	1500
10.	Water Color, 1987, mixed media on wood	825

in Picasso's use of African masks, and the native works of art that we had seen in Papua New Guinea, free from traditional Western representation. I began making color choices that better expressed my artistic self. I began experimenting with texture—putting plaster on the surface of wood panels, scraping the paint or writing in it, revealing what was underneath.

In 1988, the Connecticut Gallery in Marlboro included me in a show, "A Summer Celebration." In 1989, I showed at the Madison Gallery's "Collector's Choice." And while the nine of us continued showing our work individually, the excitement of the collaborative work engulfed us more and more.

The perfect name for the group came to us one day while we were working. Someone suggested "The Mother's Arm," and then someone else followed with "The Other's Arm." That was it. The name suggested that the completed work was being done by a tenth person, finished by "the other's arm." By collaborating we had managed to let go of our individual egos, whose absence gave a mysterious and "other" dimension to the art.

We found a new direction, making six-by-eight-inch collages, fastening Velcro on the reverse sides of the rectangles, then arranging them on Velcro-prepared walls to create a larger piece. We moved into the open second floor of an unfinished house further out in the country where we were free to prepare the walls.

By 1991, we had completed so much work that we mounted two shows simultaneously, one at Erector Square

"Eavenly Archetype," by the Collaborative, 46 x 46 inches, c. 1985

in New Haven and another at the Mellon Art Center on the campus of Choate Rosemary Hall in Wallingford. We fixed Velcro to the gallery walls and reassembled the pieces from the studio. At the Mellon Center we challenged visitors to arrange the component parts of one piece to their liking, a hands-on, interactive work of art. At Erector Square, we named one very large seven-by-four-foot piece, "The Quilt," because it reminded us of collaborative quilt-making, an art form practiced by women through the

"Corners," by the Collaborative, 31 x 36 inches, c. 1985

ages. We were pleased with both shows and again received positive feedback.

Once a month, our group visited New York museums and galleries, where we were drawn to artists who worked collaboratively. We studied Gilbert & George, an English duo, and Judy Chicago, whose "Dinner Party" has become an iconic feminist work. IRWIN, a group of five male artists from Eastern Europe, particularly interested us, because men had sometimes mentioned to

The New York Times

SUNDAY, AUGUST 17, 1986

Art by Collective,
Art by Chance

By CHARLOTTE LIBOV

EVERY Tuesday, nine artists gather at Caroline Chandler's Guilford studio to participate in an unusual lottery. They leave art to chance. Slips of paper are passed around, and each artist matches one to the piece of art she will take home. The next week, the group reconvenes and the procedure is repeated.

What happens here is highly unorthodox in the traditional world of art. Instead of pursuing their individual creative visions, these nine work collectively. Each of their collages bears the imprint of every group member who has painted and pasted over, and even destroyed, the work done before.

"Anyone who thinks of an idea as 'their' idea could never work in a group like this," said Ms. Chandler, a member of this group of artists who, under the name of "Etcetera," have been working together for the last three years.

Etcetera began when Ms. Chandler assembled a group of artists to share models in her home. Its members, who range in age from 42 to 75, had graduated from art school decades before. But they still had a thirst to learn, and discovered that banding together was a fine way to slake it.

"We call it 'our search,'" Ms. Chandler said. What evolved was a sort of mini-college, where the group informally studied modern art and various painting techniques, as well as psychology and philosophy.

"We started viewing ideas not as 'our' ideas, but viewing ourselves as vehicles to bring the ideas forth," she said.

Early on, the group decided that collage, a type of art created by the layering of materials one upon the other, was a logical medium for their collaborative work. "We started working on the large collages together," Ms. Chandler said. "Then we decided to try it with each person starting a piece at home and bringing it in, then passing it on. Then we would critique the piece, and the artist would have to defend what she had done. The purpose of that was so the artist could show she had had an honest dialogue with the work."

The women thought that their methods might be useful to other artists, so they began to document their work. Their critiques were posted, so members could study them. Pictures of works in progress were taken as well, and compiled into a scrapbook.

"It was that feeling in the pit of

Continued on Page 15

Continued From Page 1

your stomach that something significant was happening, and you wanted to record it," Ms. Chandler said.

In addition to Ms. Chandler, the group includes Sheila Kaczmarek, Dorothy Van Deusen and Joan Cornog, all of Guilford; Elizabeth Boyd, Margaret Greaves and Jane Harris, all of Madison; Doris Christie of Mystic, and Joyce Colter of Branford.

Although they work in a group as Etcetera, they also work independently at their own studios. They have all exhibited and won awards. Their strong identities as artists allow them to submerge themselves in Etcetera, Ms. Chandler said.

The artists have struggled with their share of hurt feelings and bruised egos, but have emerged the stronger, Mrs. Greaves said. "I don't want us to sound too goody-goody," she said.

"But at these sessions, anything goes," Ms. Boyd said. "You could rip off a piece of someone else's work, or cover over it, or obliterate it. There are some tears and some anger."

Collaboration began to change the group's work. Early works show huge, vivid, well-defined figures; later works are more abstract, with swirls of color, some of which merge into the background until they seem to disappear.

The group delights in doing the unexpected, and creating works that force a viewer to stop short, such as "Rift," which is composed of paint smears on corrugated cardboard. Another work entitled "What's Wrong With Your Head," has as its centerpiece a marred mirror designed to give the gazer a disjointed look, as if in an amusement park fun house.

"We used to be landscape, portrait and still-life painters; in those days, we were working on something 'out there,'" Ms. Chandler said. "Now, we've grown much more interested in the imaginative world rather than the representational. If we do a landscape, it's likely to be a landscape of a dream world, rather than something we've seen out of a window."

Although creating art is the pri-mary purpose of "Etcetera," the

The New York Times

"What's Wrong With Your Head?" by artists collective.

group also has created a strong personal bond between its members . All have families, and the question of how to juggle their lives as wives, mothers and artists has been frequently discussed.

"The things the group has dealt with are all the things necessary to deal with: death, birth, illness," Ms. Chandler said. "It's really been quite a support group."

The group has completed 51 works, and recently held its first exhibit, a show in Guilford. The group is discussing the possibility of taking the show to Boston or New York. They have also sold some pieces, which were priced from $300 to $1,000, and plan to use the money to buy a second-hand printing press, and to find shared studio space.

The women are not certain of what they will do next. "We chose the name Etcetera because it's open-ended and doesn't pin us down," Ms. Chandler said. But she is certain the collaborative work will go on. "We've been indoctrinated to believe that art has to be created by a single, struggling artist," she said. "What we're saying is there's another way." ∎

us their unwillingness to collaborate. They would comment that they could never surrender their individuality and that art came from the individual's ego, an assumption we questioned. When we met the artists of IRWIN at their opening in SoHo, they told us that in Yugoslavia, where the group had formed before the breakup of the Soviet Union, they had not even considered the possibility that art originated with individual egos. Though our collaborative groups thought alike in this respect, our approaches differed. Each artist of IRWIN had a separate role—painting, sculpting, framing, or printmaking. The

Velcro Installation at Erector Square, 1991

five did not collaborate on the same artwork, but joined forces putting a show together. We discovered one or two other collaborative attempts in New York, but none was quite like ours. The closest was the identical Starn Twins, who, of course, shared the same DNA. All of these comparisons gave us the sense that as collaborators we were on the cutting edge, that our approach was unique.

After our shows at the Mellon Center and Erector Square, our group met in my studio to discuss our next step. Energized by the sense that we were on to something new, I suggested that we take our work to New York City. We had shown in the most prestigious local venues and, to me at least, continuing to show locally seemed equivalent to standing still. But when we took a vote, I was the only

Choate Rosemary Hall Exhibition, 1991

"The Quilt," by the Collaborative, 48 x 84 inches, 1991

"Kimono," by the Collaborative, 48 x 54 inches, 1991

one who elected to move; no appeal on my part could change their minds.

The unwillingness of the others surprised me. Maybe we had not been on the same wavelength all the years we had worked together. Or perhaps some of the others did not take our art as seriously as I did. Perhaps some of their husbands had given negative feedback. Or maybe the other artists feared failure, or possibly success. The years of fruitful collaboration suddenly ended, and in 1991, The Other's Arm disbanded. For me, its dissolution was almost unbearable.

CHAPTER 19
MOVING FORWARD

Margaret's estrangement from us, Knox Jr.'s addiction, and my recovery from a badly broken ankle were difficult, but it was the dissolution of The Other's Arm that finally brought me down. The group had given me social, emotional, and artistic support for many years and its disbanding took away the final prop to my sense of well-being. Without it I collapsed into depression.

I knew that I needed help. The psychologist at Yale Medical School who evaluated me suggested talk therapy instead of medication, but when I told Knox about the recommendation he was not pleased. He sat silently like someone who had just taken a blow to the head and was waiting for a second one. I knew he had a low opinion of therapy (though not as negative as his mother's) and figured he would not approve of my seeing a therapist, but I was surprised to discover the reason for his negativity. He feared that therapy would lead to divorce, something that had happened with other couples we knew. I assured him that I was looking for a closer relationship in our marriage, not a divorce, and told him that if we could address the issues as they came up in the therapy sessions, I would make progress more quickly—which would make the therapy less expensive. He agreed, and over the next three years we discussed our Southern upbringing, our families' destructive secrets, our own feelings and needs, and our relationships with each other and our children. Each week we gained a better perspective on our lives, and Knox gained more empathy toward my need to be an artist. Although the other women in The Other's Arm had no interest in showing our work in New York galleries, I wanted to, with my own paintings. Knox, supporting me, was all for it.

⌣

In 1992, Stephen Haller accepted me into his SoHo gallery. A year later he gave me a one-person show in his beautiful new space on the top floor of 560 Broadway. SoHo at the time was the center of the New York art world, and 560 Broadway was one if its finest addresses, six floors of prestigious galleries right in the center of the action. There were moments when I thought that I must be dreaming. I was pleased with my work, encouraged because several of my paintings sold, and happy to be numbered among Haller's painters, who shared a mutual approach to color, line, texture, and other formal aspects of art. The common aesthetic gave me a sense of connection to the other gallery artists, including Judy Streeter, also from Guilford, an extremely gifted painter who became a close friend. Her death in 2001 at the tragically young age of 53 was a great personal loss to me as well as to all who knew her.

As time passed, Haller called on me to work bigger and bigger, and before long, I was painting on wooden panels that were 5 x 6', 6 x 7', and 7 x 8'. About that time, I injured my neck in a car accident, and though I continued to paint, it became physically painful to work on such large pieces. Still, I was showing in Haller's group shows and felt that things were going well, until in 1997, he began hinting that my paintings were too heavy to keep pulling out of storage. I suspected they were not selling. I was stunned and disappointed when Stephen said he was sending my unsold paintings back and was not asking for more.

I decided not to seek out another gallery in New York, but I would not stop trying to sell the work that he had returned. In 2000, the Troyer Gallery in Washington, D.C., invited me to exhibit, sold most of the large paintings left from the New York days, and continued to carry my work until the gallery closed in 2004.

Knox, inducted into the National Academy of Sciences, 1990

These were good years for Knox. At Yale he and his team of scientists continued their successful studies of the activation of muscle contraction, and in 1990, he was elected to the National Academy of Sciences, a recognition of his decades of innovative research. While the children and I were enthusiastically proud of Knox, he accepted the honor with absolute humility.

⌣

Though Knox and his mother had never resolved their conflict, their relationship improved sufficiently that Knox visited her every year in her retirement home. In 1995, I accompanied him to Dallas. Though I didn't visit Margaret, he and I went to see Elizabeth Sleeper, Aunt Meggs' daughter, who was dying of cancer. (Aunt Meggs had died three years earlier.) Elizabeth brought out two albums; one of them to my surprise and delight was the Blue Album, which I had seen only briefly 37 years earlier, the day of Knox Jr.'s baptism. This time, as I flipped through the pages, I found no newspaper clipping, but I did recall my shock at the discovery of the article with its dark secret about which the Chandler family had remained silent for decades. I thought I would never see the photos again, but Elizabeth gave the albums to me. She said, Aunt Meggs would have wanted me to have them. The gift was an omen that someday I would find the pictures of special value.

⌣

Later that year I bought the grey barn across the road with part of a small inheritance. In the mid-19th century, the barn had been built with our house but had eventually come into the hands of our next door neighbor, who kept his cows there. His widow could not afford to keep it up, and I could not bear to see it falling into ruin.

I hired a specialist in antique barns to restore it and convert it into a gallery for my paintings. The ground floor facing the road was spacious, with the original beams and a rutted, uneven floor. The land beneath the barn sloped away from the road, and under the main floor a space opened into the meadow where I had seen cows grazing when I first admired our house. The finished gallery remained rough and rustic in appearance with the structural beams still visible, but with white walls and directional lighting it became ideal for displaying art. The reconstruction took four years and cost more than I had anticipated, but when my inheritance was depleted, Knox helped me financially, knowing how I felt about historic preservation. Just as I had understood that the house in North Guilford was "meant to be" ours, the barn also seemed part of my artistic destiny.

I had studied ceramics at the Guilford Art Center and worked there as an apprentice for four years, so when we dug out a swamp behind our house to create a small pond and discovered a bed of clay, I said, "Meant to be." When we pulled out the nails that sealed off a small room in the barn and found a dug well that opened into the floor, again I said, "Meant to be." The builder transformed the lower level of the barn into a ceramics studio, with running water pumped in from the well.

My fascination with clay dated back at least to my travels with Knox to Japan, where I discovered potters carrying on the historic tradition of Korean tea bowls. These bowls were thought to possess "wabi-sabi," a quality that has been described as the material representation of Zen Buddhism. Objects with wabi-sabi have integrity and authenticity; they are true to themselves, for example, an asymmetrical bowl that reflects the hand of the artist as opposed to a manufactured bowl that is perfectly symmetrical. Wabi-sabi incorporates the beauty of nature and of humble things; it embraces imperfection and impermanence. I believe that this concept can apply to a bowl, a tea cup, or a painting, and also to a house and its furnishings. The beauty I saw in Japanese ceramics was the same beauty that drew me to New Guinean art, including the bilum bags that impressed me for their authenticity and spiritual content.

The restored barn now housed my ceramics studios and the galleries where I could show my paintings and work in clay that expressed this aesthetic. More and more I realized how important our trip to New Guinea had been, how it had changed my life and the direction of my art. About this time I began to work collaboratively again, with two women who had belonged to The Other's Arm, and I was bolstered by the feeling of art mysteriously created by group effort. We showed our work together and, in 2005, helped found the cooperative City Gallery in New Haven.

"Beyond The House" show in the barn, 2008

Knox and Caroline at the opening of an exhibit in the barn, 2011
(Photo: Betsy MacDermid)

Above: Orb, 12 inches, pinched clay, 1998
Above right: Bowl, 7 inches, dung-fired clay from our pond, 1998
Below right: Three Vessels, each 4 inches high, clay, wire, and wood, 2006

Above: "Crescent #1," 26 x 32 inches, 2011
Above right: half of "Diptych," 36 x 40 inches, 2008
Below right: "Crescent #2," 36 x 48 inches, 2010

I exhibited at the City Gallery until I began showing in my renovated barn-gallery, where I organized four shows of paintings and participated in three of ceramics between 2006 and 2011. These exhibits gave me a satisfaction I had never felt anywhere else, not even in New York, where I had just handed over my work to be framed, hung, and even priced by other people according to their preferences. When I showed my work in the barn that I had restored, across from the house that I have lived in and loved for more than 40 years, I felt wholly myself. With Knox, who was in his element as the perfect host, we gave a party-reception with wine, food, and friends for the opening of each show.

⌣

By 2004, all our children were married and Knox and I fell happily into grandparenting, welcoming nine grandchildren. During the years they were growing up, our summer reunions took place at our home, where the screened-in back porch barely accommodated the ten adults and nine grandchildren. The gatherings gave the cousins an opportunity to know each other early on and showed them where their parents had lived as children.

Later, when my art work and exhibitions demanded more of my time, we celebrated reunions and life's milestones also in Texas, and on Cape Cod. As the grandchildren ventured out into the adult world with commitments and jobs spread across the United States, it was more difficult to get everyone together. Knox and I were thankful for the healthy, intelligent, talented, and caring human beings that they were, and, although fewer and smaller gatherings were in order, we were grateful for all the good times we still had with them.

Wellfleet reunion, 2007 (Photo: Jay Elliot)

PART 4

To the living we owe some consideration. To the dead we owe nothing but the truth.
Voltaire, Letter to M. de Grenonville (1719)

CHAPTER 20
THE TRUTH

Some 50 years after the article chronicling the death of Knox's father had dropped out of the Blue Album, the tragedy that had been hovering in a dark corner of my mind finally emerged to seize my full attention. During those years my children, the demands of Knox's career, my mother's problems, and my commitment to art had fully occupied me, but in the first decade of the 21st century I could look back and see that I had achieved many of my goals. The children had grown up and found their paths in life; Knox had retired, his scientific achievements widely recognized; my work had been shown and sold in New York and Washington; I had established my own gallery and held shows there. Now I determined to find out, if I could, what happened on that day in July 1943.

Our daughter Margi, by profession a lawyer and by nature a sleuth, had begun investigating her grandfather's life and death. In 2000, she had contacted the National Archives and placed an inquiry in the *OSS Society Journal* seeking anyone who might know anything about W. K. or his death. The material from the archives was not especially informative, and six years went by before Margi's inquiry attracted attention. Then later one of Rosemary's relatives posted a query in the *OSS Society Journal*:

My great aunt Rosemary Sidley worked for the OSS and for Gen. Donovan. She was murdered by someone and Donovan apparently came to see my great-grandmother to give her the real story, which she took to her grave. Do you have any suggestions as how I could get more information about this?[1]

The writer of the inquiry knew nothing about W. K. Chandler, not even his name, only that Rosemary's family believed there was a "real story" important enough for General Donovan to have contacted Rosemary's mother in person. Margi and the relative began to correspond, both eager to investigate the mystery. The following year, however, heightened business obligations made it impossible for either of them to continue the research. Margi wanted me to take over the project, because she and three colleagues had established their own law firm, doubling her work load.

While I had no idea of the enormity of the task or the obstacles in my path, I was convinced of the importance of my mission. Early in my research I had come across the remark by Voltaire that heads this section; I took it as inspiration and justification. That was it, I thought. I owed W.K., the first Knox Chandler, nothing but the truth, and if possible, the whole truth. I hoped to discover the

1 *OSS Society Journal*, Winter, 2007, 22.

"real" story, something other than the sordid tale printed in the newspapers. I wanted to bring him back from the shadows, where he existed in people's memories only as the murderer of a pretty "former Chicago society girl." I wanted to create a portrait of a man whom I knew to be a highly intelligent scholar, a father, and a patriot who had performed a difficult service for our country. I wanted him remembered not simply for the way his life had ended, but for the things he had achieved. In making that portrait "breathe," I hoped to discover both the truth and the man.

Once again Knox encouraged me. After he retired, he had become willing to help out around the house. Previously he had taken care of the "big things" in our marriage while the little things—child care, meal preparation, and household chores—had been my territory, but now he went grocery shopping and, true to his scientific background, started making inventories of the things stored on the basement shelves and in the freezer in the barn. He took on the dishwasher and his once-in-a-while cabbage soup became a small part of a larger repertoire. For a man who had professed inability to operate a washing machine, these were giant steps forward. Truthfully, I could not have written this story without his help. My journey in writing was also his; as the two of us entered our 80s, this collaboration became an adventure for both of us.

We began culling our file cabinets for anything about his father, organizing family letters, newspaper articles, photo collections, even reading his scholarly publications. From this material I was able to sketch the outlines of his life before he joined the OSS, to document his interest in 18th-century literature and the Age of Reason, to chart his rapid academic advance from Texas, to Chicago, to Harvard, to Vanderbilt. I followed him as he moved away from small-town Brownwood with its culture of religious fundamentalism to the intellectually stimulating environment of academia.

In 2008, after material about the OSS in World War II had been declassified, I requested W. K.'s file from the National Archives. The most revealing of the documents that arrived was the *vita* that he had submitted to the OSS outlining his life history and his qualifications for service in the organization. The document contains details that no one in the family remembered, details that helped to fill out the picture of the man.

As a teenager W. K. had worked as a pipe-fitter's helper in the railroad shops where he gained "considerable amateur experience with all sorts of tools." He had toiled as a clerk in a grocery store and become secretary to the superintendent of the railroad. During World War I, he spent nine months in the infantry, where he rapidly rose from private to corporal to sergeant and finally to first sergeant, an early indication of the competence that later marked his academic career. After the war W. K. served in the U.S. Coast Guard, rising rapidly there as well, becoming one of three deck officers on the U.S.C.G. *Seminole*, and then skipper of a 75-foot patrol craft. In 1924, when the service was expanding to cope with Prohibition, he took a competitive exam for a commission; he came in eleventh from a group of several hundred and was commissioned ensign.

After his stint in the armed forces and the coast guard, W. K. worked for two years as head of the English department at Schreiner Institute, a military junior college in Kerrville, Texas. As an undergraduate at the University of Texas, he had authored an essay on Thomas Dekker's "Shoemaker's Holiday," which was published in an academic journal, and immediately after he graduated he was hired as an instructor of English at UT for one year.

After finishing his PhD at the University of Chicago, he became an instructor at Harvard where, during the summer of 1940, he took charge of the "English" program at the shortwave radio station WRUL (World Radio University for the Listener), whose educational programs promoted international understanding. The "English" program presented American opinion, "editorial and otherwise," says the *vita*, concerning the imminent war. W. K. broadcast half the programs himself and arranged for people to handle the others.

While the Chandler family insisted that W. K. did not want to join the OSS, the tone of the *vita* suggests he might have been less than totally negative. Instead of playing down his accomplishments, which he might have done if he had wanted to avoid joining, he presents himself as a man who certainly was qualified—fluent in French and Spanish, familiar with German (not to mention Latin and Greek), well-traveled, and experienced as a researcher (with more than 14 years of study in libraries in the US and abroad). He hunted and fished, knew a good deal about photography, and had experience with navigation and seamanship. In the Coast Guard, he had demonstrated his ability to lead. At several universities he had demonstrated his ability to teach.

W. K. was aware that in refusing to join the OSS, he would probably be drafted and might be pulled into combat, which seemed the greater risk. In fact, this choice, to join the OSS, seemingly of lesser risk, was to prove fatal.

⌣

Four years after having received the *vita* and other material from the National Archives, Margi and I decided to visit the archives in person, hoping to uncover something new. We met in Washington, drove out to College Park, Maryland, where the OSS material is stored, and spent two days pulling out boxes of documents and sifting through their contents. The results disappointed us because we found nothing relevant. One of the archivists suggested that we look at the minutes of the OSS Executive Committee around the time of the tragedy.

We examined copies of the declassified minutes from June 1 through October 19 of 1943. The documents— blurry photocopies of typed carbon copies—were difficult to read, but they were clear enough to see that the tragic deaths of July 12 were not mentioned. On Tuesday, July 13, the thirtieth meeting of the Executive Committee since January, the minutes, only a page and a half long, recorded the reading of the minutes of the previous meeting (July 10) and two new items of business. The first item concerned a survey report made by Research and Analysis; the second involved the allocation of space in the Army Annex Building. The brevity of these July 13 minutes surprised me, especially compared to the considerably longer records of meetings before and after that date.[2] The minutes of the following week, the thirty-first meeting of the committee, on Monday, July 19, 1943, also remained silent about the tragedy, though at subsequent meetings such insignificant problems as "lost badges" and "transportation" came up frequently.[3] I decided that any discussion of W. K.'s death had simply been destroyed, redacted, never recorded in the first place, or buried beyond hope of retrieval.

---

2 There were meetings on June 25, June 26, June 27, June 28, and June 29, around the time Lt. Col. Baker was leaving, and also on July 1, July 6, July 8, and July 10. Most of these minutes ran four or five pages in length.

3 July 20, 1943, was a Tuesday. Either the day or the date is wrong in the minutes.

VITA

William Knox Chandler

Name: William Knox Chandler

Address: (Vanderbilt University, Nashville, Tenn.)
3506 Central Avenue, Nashville, Tenn. Tel.: 8-6026

Education: Graduate Kingsville High School, Kingsville, Texas; B.A. University
of Texas; M.A., University of Texas; Ph. D., University of Chicago.
(In addition, I had, in 1917, a secretarial course at Eastman
Business College, Poughkeepsie, N.Y.)

General Experience:

1. Mechanical: I worked as a pipe-fitter's helper in the railroad shops
at Kingsville, Texas, for eight or nine months in 1916. I have had
considerable amateur experience with all sorts of tools both before
and since that time.
2. Clerical: 1) I worked as a clerk in a grocery store at Kingsville,
Texas, for six or seven months. 2) I was secretary to the superintendent of the railroad for a year and a half (before and after our entry
into the war). 3) I supported myself in large part by doing various
secretarial jobs while I was an undergraduate at the University of Texas
(a. for Mrs. Percy Pennybacker, president of the confederation of
women's clubs of America, and for, b. the sales manager of E.L. Steck
& Co., printers and lithographers; in addition, I substituted several
weeks for an ill court reporter). 4) I worked one year as an abstractor
of titles for a Guarantee Title Company in Lockhart, Texas, during an
oil boom. This job required constant searching of county records (the
early ones were in Spanish) and some small knowledge of map-making and
reading.
3. Teaching: Two years as head of the English department at Schreiner
Institute, Kerrville, Texas (a military junior college for boys); one
year as instructor in English at the University of Texas; five years
as instructor in English at the University of Chicago; six years as
instructor and assistant professor of English at Harvard University;
two years as associate professor of English at Vanderbilt University.
4. Research: Twelve or fourteen years of experience. I have worked in
various libraries -- Texas, California, Illinois, Massachusetts, New
York, London, Edinburgh. I have spent several months in sequence in
London and elsewhere. My particular research interests are in a field
which is now called the "history of ideas." I will be glad to amplify
this section.
5. Radio: During June, July, and early August of 1940 I was in charge of
the English program from WRUL in Boston. This program was designed to
present the British with American openion, editorial and otherwise,
concerning the war. At first the program was thirty minutes long, five
days a week; but this was reduced to fifteen minutes because of technical problems in connection with new power installations. I did a
considerable part, perhaps half, of the broadcasting myself, and arranged
for the other programs.

6. Travel: I have travelled extensively in the United States and Mexico; in addition, I have spent several months in England and Scotland (in 1936 and 1939), something over a month in Germany and Austria (1936), and shorter periods in Belgium and France (1936 and 1939).
7. Languages: Spanish. Until ten years ago I spoke Spanish rather fluently; I still read it with ease. French. I read French with ease, but speak it rather poorly. I was head examiner for the Harvard English Department in French. German. I read German, but not with ease, and speak it quite poorly, though adequately for purposes of travel and basic communication. Latin. I studied Latin for five years and still have a fair reading knowledge. Greek. I studied Greek for two years, and have forgotten most of what I learned.
8. Sports: I have done a good bit of hunting in Texas and Mexico; I have fished from the gulf to rather remote parts of Canada; I have played college tennis and golf.
9. Military: About nine months in the U.S. Infantry -- as private, corporal, sergeant, and first sergeant. This was when I was 18. About a year as ensign in the U.S. Coast Guard: first as one of three deck officers on the old U.S.C.G. Seminole, then as skipper of a 75-foot modification of the naval submarine chasers. To this I might add three months of instruction of Navy V-5 and V-7 candidates in navigation in the spring of this year at Vanderbilt University.

Nautical Experience:

1. Numerous one day trips in small sailing craft; numerous three-day trips on 75-foot Coast Guard patrol craft, powered by two gasoline engines; and considerable canoe experience (if the canoe is not too small to be mentioned. In addition, I was watch officer for some months on the U.S.C.G. Seminole.
2. On sailing craft, my experience was as crew; on the 75-foot patrol craft, as skipper; on the Coast Guard Cutter, as watch officer (deck).
3. My technical knowledge of engines, ship-building, designing, etc. is not at all extensive.
4. My knowledge of navigation is, I think, fairly sound, though my experience is somewhat limited. In 1924 I took a competitive examination for a commission in the U.S. Coast Guard -- an examination incident to the expansion in that service which prohibition brought about. Several hundred, I was told, took the examination (embracing piloting, seamanship, navigation, and so on), and I stood eleventh. I was commissioned Ensign, and served a few months on the Coast Guard cutter Seminole -- one of three watch officers. I was later transferred to command of a 75-footer, but resigned in March of 1925 to an academic career. Since 1925 I have retained an active interest in navigation, and have kept up moderately well with the short cuts in celestial navigation developed since 1925 (methods like those of Ageton, Dreisonstok, etc.) This spring I taught navigation at Vanderbilt University to students in V-5 and V-7. The physicist who had taught one class the first term was called into government service, and I was more or less drafted to take over his work. I taught one course in piloting, plotting, etc., and another in celestial navigation. In these courses I used the Naval Acad. textbook (Dutton's) and directed laboratories involving the use of many charts obtained from the Department of Commerce and the Hydrographic Office. I believe I could pass, and pass easily, a stiff examination on navigation, both coastwise and celestial.

CHAPTER 21

THE ORIGINS OF THE OSS

In September 1942, when W. K. Chandler arrived in Washington fresh from his teaching job at Vanderbilt, the Office of Strategic Services (OSS) was in a state of chaos. During the run-up to World War II, United States intelligence activities had been divided up among competing agencies; the Departments of State, Treasury, and War, and the Navy all provided intelligence, and each had its own policies and personnel. J. Edgar Hoover, director of the FBI since 1924, also had his finger in the pot, having secured for his agency responsibilities for domestic security, anti-espionage, and political surveillance in Latin America. President Franklin D. Roosevelt, concerned about this fragmented effort which inevitably led to turf wars and miscommunication, recognized that the Army, Navy and State Department units were underfunded and mediocre. Worse yet, the disjointed system often left him out of the loop, unaware of overseas developments. He desperately wanted a coordinated intelligence agency reporting directly to him.

In the summer of 1941, before Pearl Harbor, Roosevelt asked Colonel William J. ("Wild Bill") Donovan to draft a plan for such a coordinated intelligence service. Donovan, a hero of World War I and a well-connected Wall Street lawyer, had already traveled abroad on unofficial fact-finding missions for FDR, and in Britain he had met William Stephenson, head of British Security

Coordination in the Western Hemisphere. Impressed by the British service and recognizing the disorganized state of American intelligence, Donovan wanted to create an American counterpart, a move that Stephenson enthusiastically endorsed. Donovan submitted his plan and in July was appointed head of a new civilian intelligence organization.

On June 13, 1942, six months after Pearl Harbor, Roosevelt issued a military order creating the OSS as an agency of the Joint Chiefs of Staff charged with collecting and analyzing strategic war information and secret intelligence required for military operations, as well as conducting unspecified "special operations" not assigned to other agencies. FDR then offered Donovan the opportunity to lead the new service. Donovan, who really wanted a combat assignment, replied that he would accept only if three conditions were met: that he would report directly to the president; that his operations would be financed from a secret, unaccountable fund; and that the president would instruct other departments to allow him a free hand.[1] Roosevelt granted these requests, which guaranteed Donovan the autonomy to work outside bureaucratic channels, to hire anyone he wished, and to get funding without submitting vouchers and without scrutiny on how the money was spent. The Joint Chiefs of Staff were to give him all the help he needed, while he had the power

---

1 Douglas Waller, *Wild Bill Donovan: The Spymaster Who Created the OSS and Modern American Espionage* (New York: Free Press, 2011), 71.

and freedom to organize and run the OSS as he saw fit. To say that the rival intelligence departments within the government were unhappy with these arrangements would be an understatement. The concessions Donovan had negotiated provoked deep anger, as the other intelligence departments continued to resent Donovan's power and access to the president.

The conditions Donovan demanded before accepting the job—especially freedom from oversight of OSS spending and direct presidential access—guaranteed the OSS a high level of secrecy as well as autonomy. Because this secrecy in turn generated even more resentment, it became increasingly important for the OSS to protect its reputation from criticism and to see that its secrets remained secret. When Donovan at one point decided to court martial an incompetent officer, for example, his aides protested that a court martial of any officer for any reason would undermine the OSS's secrecy and destroy morale.[2] Donovan's enemies, especially J. Edgar Hoover, lay in wait for any opportunity to undermine the OSS.

⌣

Donovan had risen to prominence from an Irish Catholic working-class background in Buffalo, New York. Although he had attended Columbia University Law School at the

---

2 Richard Harris Smith, *OSS: The Secret History of America's First Central Intelligence Agency* (Berkeley; University of California Press, 1972), 6.

same time as the wealthy, upper-class Roosevelt, the two men did not travel in the same social circles. Nevertheless, Donovan's personality would later appeal to FDR, who as president admired the leadership ability, skills, and daring that had earned Donovan a promotion to colonel during World War I; he also liked Donovan's optimism, vision, and energy. Both Donovan and FDR were secretive by nature, attracted to undercover tactics, and open to risky ideas.[3] Both men were willing, even eager, to work outside official channels. Donovan would later say that FDR was a "real cloak-and-dagger boy"; FDR would refer to Donovan as "my secret legs."[4]

As a recruiter Donovan sought out risk-takers and creative thinkers who were prepared to disobey orders, in short, men like himself. He hired mob bosses and safecrackers, movie stars, socialites, and jujitsu masters, but he also recruited distinguished academics including historians from Yale, Harvard, and Princeton. He signed up people who had traveled abroad, people fluent in foreign languages and informed about foreign affairs. Many were chosen through personal contact, some even by hearsay. J. Edgar Hoover called them mere amateurs. The ideal OSS candidate was described, jokingly perhaps, as a PhD who could win a bar fight. Given Donovan's emphasis on rule-breaking and innovation, it is not surprising that he paid

---

3 Waller, *Wild Bill Donovan*, 104-5.

4 Waller, *Wild Bill Donovan*, 70, 77.

little attention to background checks or the psychological fitness of the recruits, actions that would not be instituted officially until 1944, partly in reaction to W. K.'s death.

⌣

In December 1941, even before the OSS was officially chartered, Donovan recognized the need for a centralized school to train the men who would become operatives and the teachers who would instruct them. He called in Joseph R. Hayden and Kenneth H. Baker and explained what he wanted. Hayden, a former professor of political science at the University of Michigan, had been vice-chancellor of the Philippines during the 1930s. Baker, a professor of psychology at Ohio State University, had previously been recruited for the Research and Analysis (R&A) branch.

The conversation during the meeting, recorded in the typescript that forms the basis of the *History of the Schools and Training Branch*, gives an idea of Donovan's personality and of the difficulties the training schools would face:

> "I want you to start the schools," he [Donovan] said.
>
> One of the men wondered, "What schools?"
>
> "The SI [Secret Intelligence] training schools," Donovan answered.
>
> "But we don't know anything about

espionage schools," came the reply.

"Who does?" said Donovan, cutting off any argument. [5]

General Donovan was correct when he said that no Americans, including Hayden and Baker, had experience in setting up or operating schools to train spies, saboteurs, or guerilla fighters, but as professors both Hayden and Baker knew about teaching, about devising, organizing, and presenting course material.

As long as the US had remained neutral, Donovan had been reluctant to start training men for sabotage, espionage, and other special operations, but in September 1941, the British, already at war with Germany, had decided to build a camp in Canada modeled on the training schools in England. It was called Camp X and was situated on a sparsely inhabited piece of shoreline on Lake Ontario, about an hour east of Toronto. Camp X would train commandos and provide the British with propaganda to get American cooperation in British subversive activities.[6] Its

---

5 *History of the Schools and Training Branch, Office of Strategic Services,* William L. Cassidy, editor (San Francisco, Calif.: Kingfisher Press, 1983), 37. This study of the training schools, originally a report written in 1945, was declassified in 1981 and 1985 and obtained by Cassidy through a Freedom of Information Act query.

6 John Whiteclay Chambers II, *OSS Training in the National Parks and Service Abroad in World War II* (Washington, D.C.: U.S. National Park Service, 2008), 50. Chambers's history is online at https://www.nps.gov/parkhistory/online_books/oss., 50.

half dozen buildings were completed in December 1941, and the place opened two days after Pearl Harbor, serving not only as a model for OSS training camps but as a site where many Americans were actually trained. Among the British intelligence agents trained there was Ian Fleming, who later wrote the James Bond 007 novels.

The first Americans attended Camp X in February 1942, taking a basic month-long course. In March, Kenneth Baker went to the camp to observe the latest techniques for training secret agents and saboteurs.[7]

The program was brutal. It included physical conditioning—five-mile runs by day and night, obstacle courses conducted under simulated or real gunfire, parachute jumping, and instruction in hand-to-hand combat—killing with knives, guns, or bare hands. Trainees also learned subversive skills—developing and maintaining a false identity, writing and decoding ciphers, and so on. The training sought to toughen men mentally and physically for the violent acts they would later perform, to teach them the survival skills they would need behind enemy lines, and to bolster their self-confidence. In April, Baker brought back to Washington the complete syllabus, "the bible," of Camp X, which would become the model for the American curriculum during the early years of OSS training. Some of the instructors at the Canadian facility also moved to the US to hasten the training process.

---

7 David Stafford, *Camp X* (New York: Pocket Books, 1986), 66.

One of these was British officer William Fairbairn, "Dangerous Dan," the former assistant commissioner of the Shanghai Municipal Police Command, whose mastery of Asian martial arts was legendary. He had fought Chinese street gangs and drug smugglers, held off rioters, and invented a razor-sharp, double-edged stiletto thin enough to slide between the ribs and long enough to penetrate thick clothing. Even without a knife Fairbairn knew a hundred ways to disable or kill an enemy with his hands, his feet, a broken bottle, or anything at hand.[8] Because the OSS stressed the physical prowess, self-confidence, and self-reliance needed on hazardous missions, instruction in close-combat techniques, armed and unarmed, was a major component of the training. Fairbairn taught in Britain and Canada and then worked for the OSS from 1942 to 1945 when he was in his late 50s. Lean and taciturn, fanatically dedicated to his craft, Fairbairn had, according to one of his students, "an honest dislike of anything that smacked of decency in fighting."[9]

Hayden soon dropped out of the training program, and the burden of educating operatives fell on Baker, who in June 1942, had become head of the Special Intelligence training school and in January 1943, head of the Schools

8 Chambers, *OSS Training in the National Parks*, 191. A shorter version of this study appeared as "OSS Training during World War II," *Studies in Intelligence*, vol. 54, no. 2 (June 2010).

9 Stafford, *Camp X*, 78.

and Training Branch of the OSS.[10] In the middle of this period—in September 1942—W. K. Chandler was recruited to carry out research for the OSS. It was Baker who moved W. K. Chandler from research to training, and who would become his mentor at the "Farm."

—

Kenneth Baker was instrumental in establishing the "Farm" on the model of British spy schools in rural England and Scotland. Located on an estate of about 100 acres near Clinton, Maryland, about 20 miles south of Washington, the area had been called Lothian Farm when it was owned by a Pittsburgh industrialist; it was secluded, with a main house, outbuildings, and even a swimming pool. It opened in May 1942, headed by Baker, with a class of eight trainees, who were taught safecracking, bribery, recruiting and handling agents, concealment, and the construction of cover stories. Later courses included map reading, pistols, and small arms.[11] Curious neighbors were told that the property was a headquarters for a few Army officers and would be used for testing military "gadgets."[12] It had a library of documents and books, as well as equipment

10 *History of the Schools and Training Branch*, 48.

11 Chambers, *OSS Training in the National Parks*, 67.

12 *History of the Schools and Training Branch*, 43.

for showing Army and Navy training films. Baker's wife acted as house manager and there was a staff of six, plus two secretaries. By November 1942, as the training schools were repeatedly re-organized, it had become the advanced Secret Intelligence School.

Although the "Farm," officially known as RTU-11 (rural training unit), was civilian in style and seemed low-key, it was not free from the tensions that had troubled the OSS since the beginning. Other government agencies with intelligence roles remained hostile to the OSS. Even within the OSS, which was struggling to centralize and streamline its educational facilities, there was infighting as the OSS operational branches (those devoted to sabotage, espionage, and so on) wanted to retain control of their own trainees and curricula.

Baker was in a difficult position. He was a professor, and though he had been in the military reserves, he alienated career officers simply because he was not one of them. He was a poor record keeper and sometimes went out of official channels to get supplies quickly, further angering those who stayed within the guidelines. Donovan got him a commission as a lieutenant colonel to help his relations with the Army, but it was too little too late.

At the same time, the armed forces were preparing for the invasion of France, which would take place in 1944. In the spring of 1943, as the OSS began recruiting large numbers of trainees who in turn required more teachers, the stresses on the training program escalated. Baker was forced out in June 1943, leaving the "Farm" understaffed and in disarray.[13] W. K. Chandler, now chief instructor, found himself under intense pressure.

---

13 Chambers, *OSS Training in the National Parks*, 69.

CHAPTER 22
A SCHOOL FOR SPIES

Like all OSS recruits, W. K. Chandler received basic training that was both physical and psychological, designed to prepare men for operations that they would conduct behind enemy lines. During the period in 1942 when W. K. first arrived in Washington, he adopted a "cover," which his fellow trainees were instructed to penetrate. According to his wife he posed as a "man of the church," a choice that followed the principle that a man's cover should reflect a familiar way of life, down to its speech patterns and wardrobe. Margaret Chandler believed that her husband maintained his role so successfully that none of his fellow students saw through his disguise.

It is uncertain whether W. K. received further training in the US or at Camp X, but it is highly likely that he attended Camp X, since Americans were still being trained there in the autumn of 1942. Whether in the US or Canada, W. K. would have received instruction in brutal fighting, survival skills, and subversive activities. His first actual assignment, however, demanded none of these skills, but drew on his experience as a professor. The recruits of Research and Analysis, one of the earliest and most successful branches of the OSS, had been selected mostly from leading universities. The researchers used publicly available information—from newspapers, libraries (including the Library of Congress), government documents and business sources—to assess the weaknesses and strengths of the Axis powers and provide material to support Allied military actions in the field.[1] Among the academics were historians, anthropologists, economists, geographers, and at least one professor of English literature. W. K., with his years of research experience, was well suited to the job.

As his wife was later told, his work focused on North Africa where Operation Torch, the Allied invasion, would take place in November 1942. He apparently succeeded brilliantly at this work, for after his death his OSS recruiter, Major Harold J. Coolidge, wrote that during his months doing research, W. K. worked rapidly and energetically, turning out results with such efficiency that his superiors often had to seek additional assignments for him.[2] It is generally thought that the contributions of the OSS played an important role in ensuring the success of the American invasion of Vichy French North Africa.[3] W. K.'s accomplishments might have been instrumental in

---

1 Edward Hymoff, *The OSS in World War II*, rev. ed. (New York: Richardson & Steirman, 1986), 78. https://www.cia.gov/news-information/featured-story-archive/2010-featured-story-archive/oss-research-and-analysis.html.

2 Harold J. Coolidge, undated letter to Margaret Chandler.

3 Office of the Assistant Secretary for War, *The Overseas Targets: War Report of the OSS*, Vol. 2 (New York: Walker & Co., 1976), 18-19. Cited in Chambers, *OSS Training in the National Parks*, 584; www.nps.gov/parkhistory/online_ books/oss/chap11.pdf.

his eventual transfer to the training schools, specifically to the "Farm."

In January 1943, several months after he began working in R&A, W. K. took the oath of office, swearing to uphold the Constitution. At the request of Kenneth Baker, who had also worked in R&A but was now head of the training schools, he moved from his research job and became chief instructor of the Special Intelligence school at the "Farm." The position required a whole set of different abilities and carried new responsibilities. No longer did W. K. collect and analyze information, a task for which his command of foreign languages and academic background qualified him. Now he was a teacher as he had been in the past, but at the "Farm" he was faced with introducing course material almost as unfamiliar to him as it was to his students: he knew only what his own training and the British curriculum had provided. Yet his students' lives might depend on what he passed on to them. And in fact one of the criticisms that students leveled against the training schools was that the instructors, at least in this early period, had little or no training in the field.

In the spring of 1943, around Easter, when W. K. had been in Washington for about seven months and at the "Farm" for about three, he brought his family from Texas to join him. Margaret and the children stopped in Boston on their way, perhaps to visit old friends from the couple's Harvard days, continuing to Maryland, where they settled in a small house in Clinton, close to the "Farm."

On at least one occasion, W. K. brought Knox to the "Farm." Knox was disappointed, as any nine-year-old would be, that he could not swim in the pool (he remembers people using it during his visit), but he was given a couple of the black molded-resin airplane models he had seen hanging from a ceiling, models used to teach trainees to identify enemy aircraft. Knox was also allowed to practice on the shooting range with the .22 rifle that W. K. had given him in advance of his tenth birthday, a rite of passage for a Texas boy. Given that the "Farm" was a secret training camp, it is strange that his father would bring him there or would let him practice on the official range, but Knox clearly remembered the incident.

⌣

In August 1942, a month before W. K. took up his job with R&A, Rosemary Sidley, eager to help in the war effort, arrived in Washington. A 31-year-old divorcée, she was tall (five feet eight inches) and slender (128 pounds), with brown hair, hazel eyes, and an olive complexion.[4]

Rosemary had been born in 1911 to a prominent Chicago family. Her mother, Irene Sidley, was a social leader whose comings and goings, volunteer activities, and even wardrobe choices were mentioned in the society sections of the Chicago newspapers. In addition, Irene was

---

4 OSS job application form: Rosemary Sidley, National Archives II (RG 226) 230 86 40 6 Box 709.

known for her business and leadership skills. She served as executive director of the Red Cross Gray Ladies and also headed an interior decorating firm. Her reputation as a decorator earned her a position on a symposium panel to discuss whether modern architecture and interiors were "conducive to livable American homes." The other panelists included three noteworthy Chicago architects, one of whom was Frank Lloyd Wright.[5] Mrs. Sidley traveled extensively in Europe, sometimes taking Rosemary. Her social connections led to business commissions; in 1930, for example, Irene Sidley Antiques/Interiors had provided the furnishings for a new clubhouse of the North Shore Golf Club on Lake Winnebago in Wisconsin at a cost of $14,000, a large sum at the time.[6] During the winter Rosemary and her mother lived on Pearson Street on Chicago's Gold Coast; they spent their summers in the exclusive suburb of Highland Park.

Rosemary attended the University School for Girls in Chicago and later transferred to Rosemary Hall (the similarity in names is coincidental), a private girls' school in Greenwich, Connecticut. She completed the fifth form (roughly equivalent to the eleventh grade), but did not graduate, for reasons that are not known. With

---

5 *Chicago Tribune*, May 5, 1932, http://archives.chicagotribune.com/1932/05/05/page/13/article/elizabeth-galt-will-be-bride-in-west-today.

6 http://www.nsgolfclub.com/history-6.html.

her education and travels, she became fluent in French.[7] When she was 18, she came out as a debutante. Two years later at a friend's wedding, she caught the bridal bouquet and ten months after that, as tradition suggested, she was the first of the bridesmaids to marry. Rosemary and her beau, Charles Ingram Bernard III, eloped to Waukegan, north of Chicago, arriving at the police station at midnight and asking for a marriage license. A justice of the peace, probably rousted out of bed, came to the station, took them to his house, issued them a license, and performed a ceremony. The bride was 20 years old; the groom, some years her senior, was recently divorced, his wife having claimed desertion.[8]

The Bernards moved to New York. For about six months from August 1932 until January 1933, Rosemary worked as a secretary for the National Economy League, an organization dedicated to providing non-partisan opposition to "outstanding governmental wastes, notably the overbearing amounts of bonus and other payments made to war veterans of other than deserving character."[9] She then worked for R. H. Macy and Company until July, leaving the position because of "family illness," according

---

7 Rosemary Sidley, National Archives II (RG 226) 230 86 40 6 Box 709.

8 Stanley Chipman, "Heiress Caught a Thorny Bouquet," *Chicago Sun*, July 15, 1943.

9 Anonymous, "The National Economy League," *Harvard Crimson*, October 14, 1932, http://www.thecrimson.com/article/1932/10/14/the-national-economy-league-pthe-national/.

to her job application for government service, from which much of this information is taken.[10] The application lists no further employment until January 1937, when she was working at the New York office of Katzenbach and Warren, Inc., a company that manufactured high-end wallpaper and fabrics. The same year she divorced her husband, telling the judge of the circuit court in Waukegan that Bernard was "too cruel to be a husband."[11] The government job application is silent about her activities during the years between 1934 and 1937.

By the autumn of 1938, after her divorce, Rosemary was again living with her mother in Chicago, working for Marshall Field and Company as an interior decorator. Wanting to help in the war effort, she went to Washington in the summer of 1942 to apply for a secretarial job with the government, moving into a small historic house in Georgetown with Barbara Soule, née Wendell, who made her debut in Chicago society the same season as Rosemary. After two divorces Soule distinguished herself in journalism and as a researcher for such notables as Arthur M. Schlesinger Jr. and George Ball, diplomat and banker.[12] Their friendship suggests the circles in which Rosemary traveled.

---

10 Rosemary Sidley, National Archives II (RG 226) 230 86 40 6 Box 709.

11 Chipman, "Heiress Caught a Thorny Bouquet."

12 Kerr, Barbara Wendell, death notice *New York Times*, August 10, 2014.

Rosemary's job application included a medical report that mentioned an appendectomy scar and a police report that noted a five-dollar speeding ticket in 1931. Her elopement as described in the Chicago newspaper suggests that she was daring.

Rosemary seemed a perfect candidate for the OSS, whose ideal female recruit was once described as "a cross between a Smith College graduate, a Powers model, and a Katie Gibbs secretary."[13] Cultured, attractive, and upper class, she fell short only in her secretarial skills and had to retake the government shorthand test before she passed.

She took the oath of office, swearing secrecy on August 6, 1942, and was classified as an assistant clerk stenographer with the grade of CAF-3 and a salary of $1620 a year.[14] As a stenographic assistant, Rosemary took on duties including classifying incoming mail, transcribing material from highly confidential and secret dispatches, sorting and routing outgoing mail. The position was modest, but it gave her access to secret information. Rosemary rose rapidly within the organization, receiving several promotions and pay raises within her first three

---

13 Elizabeth P. McIntosh, *Sisterhood of Spies: The Women of the OSS* (Annapolis, MD.: Naval Institute Press, 1998), 14. During the 1940s and later, the Katharine Gibbs Secretarial Schools turned out well-groomed, socially polished secretaries expert in typing and shorthand.

14 CAF is the abbreviation for military grades categorized as clerical, administrative, and fiscal. Rosemary was assigned to the Special Activities/B section (SA/B). The section, after various reorganizations of the training schools, would be one of the precursors of RTU-11.

months, moving up the ladder more swiftly than the official government guidelines permitted.[15] By the following April she had jumped from CAF-5 to CAF-7, junior administrative assistant with a salary of $2600, a higher security clearance, and dramatically altered duties. In her new position, according to her official job description, she dealt with important interchanges from all over the world, carried out assignments that required personal contact with high-ranking officials of other government agencies, attended secret conferences with her supervisor, took confidential and technical dictation about intelligence operations, and maintained secret progress reports about projects of the Special Activities branch of the OSS, whose work included espionage and guerilla warfare. As a junior administrative assistant, Rosemary had access to highly secret information and to highly placed government officials. In June 1943, she was appointed W. K. Chandler's assistant.[16]

⌣

In January 1943, Schools and Training had been officially established as a separate branch of the OSS under Kenneth Baker, who was responsible only to General Donovan. That same month Baker appointed W. K. chief instructor

---

15 CAF Federal Employee Guide on Promotion, Civil Service Leader, Vol. 5, No. 51, August 29, 1944.

16 Rosemary Sidley, National Archives II (RG 226) 230 86 Box 709.

of the Special Intelligence school, the "Farm." From that point, things deteriorated for W. K. In late June, Baker, whose background was civilian rather than military and who was often at odds with military intelligence personnel, had been temporarily relieved of his duties at the "Farm" and had taken leave to attend the staff school at Fort Leavenworth, Kansas. Later he would be ousted from the training schools altogether. Many of the "Farm's" best instructors had been sent overseas to start training schools abroad, and the rush of new recruits placed additional stress on those instructors remaining stateside. Although Baker had originally thought his work would involve schooling a small but professional group of undercover operators, the need for agents became so urgent as the war progressed that operatives were recruited by the hundreds. Not surprisingly the organization of the training program proved inadequate.

The departure of Baker, W. K.'s mentor, seriously ratcheted up the already increasing pressure on the chief instructor. In the early summer of 1943, W. K.'s associates noticed changes in his behavior. His wife later recalled that he was fatigued and had trouble sleeping, that he felt he had to be on call at any hour of the day or night for any one of his students who might need him. W. K.'s second-in-command, Robert Enders, who disapproved of alcohol, saw him drinking beer during the day, something disturbingly different from his usual conduct. According to his family, W. K. was in an auto accident toward the end of June and walked away from the crash site, perhaps afraid that his affiliation with a secret government agency would be discovered.[17] All of this suggests the toll that his increasingly stressful job was taking as well as his sense of responsibility to the men he was training.

---

17 Although Dr. Enders had told Knox and me in 1984 that there had been no auto accident, the author of the *History of the Schools and Training Branch*, writing in 1945, corroborates the family's recollection that there was an accident. *History of the Schools and Training Branch*, 63.

Standard Form No. 47
Approved by the Bureau
of the Budget
May 15, 1941

PERSONNEL AFFIDAVIT

Office of Strategic Services   Special Activities   Washington, D. C.
(Department or agency)   (Bureau or division)   (Place of employment)

Name   Rosemary   Sidley

(Given name, initial or initials, if any, and last name. Print or type)

Section 9A of Public 252—76th Congress, approved August 2, 1939, otherwise known as the "Hatch Act," provides:

"(1) It shall be unlawful for any person employed in any capacity by any agency of the Federal Government, whose compensation, or any part thereof, is paid from funds authorized or appropriated by any Act of Congress, to have membership in any political party or organization which advocates the overthrow of our constitutional form of government in the United States.

"(2) Any person violating the provisions of this section shall be immediately removed from the position or office held by him, and thereafter no part of the funds appropriated by any Act of Congress for such position or office shall be used to pay the compensation of such person;"

It is provided in various appropriation acts that no part of the funds so appropriated shall be used to pay the salary or wages of any person who advocates, or who is a member of an organization that advocates, the overthrow of the Government of the United States by force or violence, and that an affidavit shall be considered *prima facie* evidence that the person making the affidavit does not advocate, and is not a member of an organization that advocates, the overthrow of the Government of the United States by force or violence. Such acts provide further that any person who advocates, or who is a member of an organization that advocates, the overthrow of the Government of the United States by force or violence and accepts employment, the salary or wages for which are paid from any such appropriation, shall be guilty of a felony and, upon conviction, shall be fined not more than $1,000 or imprisoned for not more than 1 year, or both, and that the above penalty shall be in addition to, and not in substitution for, any other provisions of existing law.

*   *   *   *   *   *   *

I, ___Rosemary Sidley___ , do solemnly swear (or affirm) that I have read and understand the foregoing; that I do not advocate the overthrow of the Government of the United States by force or violence; that I am not a member of any political party or organization that advocates the overthrow of the Government of the United States by force or violence; and that during such time as I am an employee of the Federal Government, I will not advocate nor become a member of any political party or organization that advocates the overthrow of the Government of the United States by force or violence.

Rosemary Sidley
(Signature of employee)

Subscribed and sworn to before me this **6th** day of _____August_____ A. D., 19 **42**,

at __Washington, D. C.__ , _____
(City or place)   (State)

Sylvia O'Carlson
Notary Public

[SEAL]

U. S. GOVERNMENT PRINTING OFFICE : 1940— O

Standard Form No. 8
(Approved by the President, May 22, 1935)

OATH OF OFFICE

Prescribed by Section 1757, Revised Statutes of the United States

Office of Strategic Services
(Department or Establishment)

Special Activities
(Bureau or Office)

I, **Rosemary Sidley**, do
(Name in full, printed or typed)

solemnly swear (or affirm) that I will support and defend the Constitution of the
United States against all enemies, foreign and domestic; that I will bear true faith and
allegiance to the same; that I take this obligation freely, without any mental reserva-
tion or purpose of evasion; and that I will well and faithfully discharge the duties of
the office on which I am about to enter. So HELP ME GOD.

Rosemary Sidley
(Signature of Appointee)

Subscribed and sworn to before me this **6th** day of **August**, A.D. 19 **42**

at **Washington, D. C.**,
(City or place)   (State)

[SEAL]

Sylvia W. Carlson
Notary Public

NOTE.—If the oath is taken before a Notary Public the date of expiration of his commission should be shown.

My commission expires: **12/21/46**

Position to which appointed **Assistant Clerk-Stenographer CAF-3 $1620 per annum**

Date of entrance on duty **August 6, 1942**

U. S. GOVERNMENT PRINTING OFFICE   10—1889

Rosemary Sidley's Personal Affidavit and Oath of Office

CHAPTER 23
THE TRAGEDY

On the evening of July 12, 1943, W. K. Chandler drove home from the "Farm" in the government car that Kenneth Baker had previously authorized him to use. Telling his wife that he was being sent on a secret mission, W. K. gave her some money and the gold watch he had inherited from his father. He kissed his sons good night and told Knox as he tucked him into bed that he was going away for a while. Knox remembers that he carried a small suitcase. From his bedroom Knox heard his parents arguing in the next room and then the sound of the front door closing. He never saw his father again.

From here on, my narrative of the evening's events is informed guesswork, pieced together mainly from the newspaper stories that described the tragedy. At some point W. K. called Rosemary's house, where she now lived with Elizabeth Maguire, another OSS employee. When Elizabeth picked up the phone, W. K. told her he was being transferred away from Washington and wanted to say goodbye to Rosemary. Elizabeth replied that Rosemary was not home, but said he could come and wait for her.

W. K. drove to Georgetown. He parked in the street in front of Rosemary's house and went to the door. Elizabeth let him in. Rosemary had not returned. They chatted, and he mentioned again that he was going overseas; he seemed calm, and Elizabeth noticed nothing unusual about his behavior. A few minutes later Rosemary came home. She and W. K. began talking quietly. Sensing that they wanted to be alone, Elizabeth went upstairs and started to take a bath. While she was in the tub she heard three shots, a scream, and then a fourth shot. Too frightened to go downstairs and investigate, she ran to a window and shouted for help. The neighbors called the police.[1]

When the police arrived they found Rosemary's body, a fatal gunshot wound in her chest. Chandler had died with a single shot to his head, the bullet lodging in one of the walls. In his hand was the .32 caliber automatic that had killed them both. In his coat pocket were four more cartridges for the gun. When the police checked the car that Chandler had parked in the street, they found a .38 caliber automatic and a commando knife with brass knuckles on the handle, probably part of the weaponry he had been issued during his OSS training.

~

1 Maguire's account, cited in the *Washington Post* from an interview with the coroner a few days later, is the only report dating back to the time immediately after the murder that I have been able to discover; see "Coroner's Finding of Murder Ends Probe of Sidley Death," *Washington Post*, July 14, 1943. If there were other contemporary accounts, they have been lost or destroyed. My husband wrote to the Washington police department in 2013 requesting a report of his father's death, but was told the police did not keep reports longer than 50 years. His queries in the *OSS Society Journal* also went unanswered.

The story hit the newspapers the next day, with new details added as the days passed. On July 13, 1943, the *Washington Post* ran a piece that identified the victims by name and mentioned that both worked for the OSS. A detective sergeant from the homicide squad, Dave Ennis, repeated Elizabeth Maguire's story to the reporters, while two policemen from the Seventh Precinct noted that the shooting followed a "jealous argument," though the published versions of Maguire's interviews with the police and the coroner did not mention a quarrel. The two precinct policemen added that Miss Sidley had been "extremely popular."

A follow-up story on July 14, also in the *Washington Post*, added that two love letters from Chandler had been found by Sergeant Ennis "in Miss Sidley's belongings." By July 15, the *Post* had filled in some background facts. Miss Sidley came from a wealthy and socially prominent Chicago family; Chandler had been an associate professor of English at Vanderbilt. The newspaper story added that he "wrote letters of tormented conflict telling of his desire... a single one" of which was given to the press "by police yesterday" (i.e. July 14).

On July 15, the *Chicago Daily Tribune* ran its own piece that included comments from Rosemary's friends and fellow workers, to whom she claimed she had joined the OSS because it was "the first assignment offered her."[2]

---

2 "How Rejected Suitor Killed Chicago Ex-Deb," *Chicago Daily Tribune*, July 15, 1943.

In the *Tribune's* version of Elizabeth Maguire's story, Maguire "knew" that Rosemary had rejected Chandler's advances and didn't want to see him, but she agreed to let him come over "at his insistence." Some of Rosemary's friends added that "she had paid no attention to him after learning he was married." The same story reports that a search uncovered a letter from Chandler as well as "many interoffice memos" from him to her, though no other account mentions the memos or the second letter cited by the *Washington Post* on July 14. The *Tribune* story also mentions that police found "a lighted cigarette still clutched in [Rosemary's] fingers," though earlier accounts did not mention a cigarette.

Even the *New York Times* got in on the act, though their article added little new except an inaccurate comment that Rosemary had possibly inherited part of the Horlick's malted milk fortune. Dr. James Sidley, Rosemary's uncle, had married Maybelle Horlick, but Rosemary was not in line for the fortune. The *New York Times* also noted that "there was no immediate explanation why she had been working as a stenographer," because it was assumed Rosemary was a wealthy woman; the *Times* mentioned that the police gave out information of a "jealous argument," information that the *Washington Post* had published on July 13.[3] Both the *Chicago Sun* and the *Chicago Daily Tribune*, on July 15, picked up Maguire's statement that

---

3 "Man Kills Heiress Then Self in Capital: W. K. Chandler and Miss Sidley of Chicago Had Jealous Quarrel," *New York Times*, July 15, 1943.

Chandler and Sidley spoke "casually," until Miss Maguire realized that they wanted to be alone.[4]

News of the tragedy, with its overtones of money, social standing, and passion traveled as far as Florida, where the *St. Petersburg Times* reported that at "the usually staid and sober offices of the government's most secret agency, the office of strategic services, last night memos were being culled for clues to the one-way love affair murder-suicide of two of its employees."[5]

The newspapers differed in their details, one saying that Chandler shot himself under the arm, while the rest claimed he shot himself in the head, but despite these discrepancies of fact, all the headlines seized on the most lurid aspects of the crime, portraying W. K. Chandler as a jealous, rejected lover: "How Rejected Suitor Killed Chicago Ex-Deb" (*Chicago Daily Tribune*, July 15, 1943) and "Letter Tells Vain Quest for Love of Society Beauty," (*Chicago Sun*, July 15, 1943). The *Washington Post* printed the one surviving letter in its entirety on July 15 under the headline "Stenographer Slain by Supervisor When She Repulsed Advances Was Socialite-Heiress:"

Thank you again for letting me take you to lunch today. Perhaps, I made very little

---

4 *Chicago Daily Tribune*, op. cit. "Suitor Slays North Shore Heiress, Self: Letter Tells Vain Quest for Love of Society Beauty," *Chicago Sun*, July 15, 1943.

5 *St. Petersburg Times*, July 15, 1943.

sense—perhaps my attempted explanation made no more sense to you than Coleridge made at [the] time to Byron (remember Byron's [lines], "and Coleridge explaining metaphysics to the nation. I wish he would explain his explanation!") but it was a great relief to me.[6] I know that I can sleep tonight because you are you, the lovely Rosemary whom I have admired, respected, loved and still admire, respect and love. I have said horrid things in anger but not in hate: I have done still more horrid things. But the only important emotion—however different its manifestations—that has guided me for six months, now Rosemary, has been my love for you. That is the most that I can say: it is the highest compliment I can pay you or anyone else. I am not now and never will be ashamed of that love, although I am abysmally ashamed of the way I have acted. It is right for you to know this, since I have said and done what I have said and done. It is also right for you to know that I love you for these qualities among others: your

---

6 In his dedication to his satiric epic *Don Juan*, Byron mocked several contemporary poets, including Coleridge, whom he criticized for his discussions of obscure philosophy (i.e., "explaining metaphysics to the nation"). Only someone well versed in the history of English literature would have understood the reference.

essential and basic honesty, your complete loyalty, your quick and agile intelligence, your sensitiveness, your wit, your charm. This reads like a catalogue and is just as unsatisfactory as one, for it is not by adding these things together that I came to love you but by sensing the harmony of the combination in you—a harmony that adds to each quality while tending at the same time to submerge each quality in the rich and lovable fabric that is your personality. It is because I know you are all these things that I know that you will forgive me for what I have done. You do not understand how the flaming hell of uncertainty left me little peace and at times no control. You will understand and forgive because you are you. I do not deserve this much and I have no right to ask it; I have nevertheless a firm belief that you will forgive.

But I want much more, I want your love, I want your faith that once uncertainty is removed the torment, the jealousy, the turmoil will all vanish, and that the same complete trust and calm, unshakable confidence in you will appear that I have always had in your abilities, in your work, a trust and confidence that is a serene and happy thing. Think, Rosemary, think: the things you have disliked and despised in me would all disappear! No miracle is needed, just the removal of uncertainty— the nightmare, the abnormality. Normally, I am kind, I am truthful, I am loyal; I am not jealous, but loving and trustful. Believe this darling.

Sometimes books say that greater love grows out of conflict and trouble than out of placid experience. Can't this be true once? If it only could be there would be no more trouble, no more conflicts.

This is a love letter Rosemary—the first I have ever written you wholly as such. No matter what you feel, no matter what your reaction, I am glad I have written it, I ask for nothing in return; but O Rosemary, I hope, I hope.[7]

Although the newspapers found in this letter confirmation of W. K.'s mad and unrequited love for Rosemary, I found in it evidence of his deteriorating state of mind, his overwhelming sense of guilt, and his personal torment, which, in conjunction with other pieces of information would lead me to consider other interpretations of the crime.

---

7 "Stenographer Slain by Supervisor When She Repulsed Advances Was Socialite-Heiress," *Washington Post*, July 15, 1943.

Almost 70 years after the tragedy, I visited the house where the deaths had taken place. My lawyer daughter Margi and I had gone to Washington to investigate the recently declassified OSS files, and on a whim we decided to find Rosemary's house. It was a glorious November day, warm and sunny, as we walked along Georgetown's charming cobbled streets. I let my imagination drift back through time, envisioning the people who once lived in the beautiful 19th-century row houses. We turned a corner and headed down a steep hill, and there on our left was the house, painted a soft yellow instead of the white it had been in 1943. As we stood in front of the building snapping pictures with our cell phones, a woman approached us through the courtyard. We explained the reason for our curiosity, and she generously invited us in.

The house in its general feeling reminded me of our home in Guilford. Inside the door from the courtyard and directly in front of us along the far wall was a staircase. On the right, toward the street, was what must have been the front parlor where according to Elizabeth Maguire's report W. K. had waited for Rosemary to come home. On the second floor were two bedrooms whose bathrooms shared a tub that could be closed off from either side. The parlor, the stairs, and especially the tub disturbed me in a way I had not expected; I could imagine Elizabeth climbing the stairs, getting into the tub and taking a bath, suddenly terrified by the sound of gunshots and her friend's anguished scream.

Years later I located two of Elizabeth's nieces. The older one told me in a telephone conversation that Elizabeth had been too panicked to go downstairs until the bodies had been removed and that once she left the house, she never returned. She went away to recuperate emotionally, but remained traumatized for the rest of her life, never speaking of the incident to anyone, not even to the younger niece whom she later adopted.

There is one more bizarre tale about the house. After Elizabeth Maguire moved out, burdened by memories, the place came onto the rental market. Decent housing was almost unobtainable in Washington during the war, and would-be tenants jumped at any opportunity. First to apply was Roald Dahl, later to become famous as a writer but during the war officially a military attaché, though in fact he was passing information to the British secret service. Apparently, Dahl signed the lease so quickly that he failed to notice the bullet holes in the wall and the bloodstains on the carpet. When he realized what he was looking at, he turned the lease over to friends.

This anecdote is interesting partly because of what it tells us of Roald Dahl, whose fairy tales would later frighten and delight generations of children, but also because of what it tells us about the crime. If we can believe a letter that Susan Mary Patten (later Susan Alsop) wrote to columnist Joe Alsop, news about the tragedy was common knowledge among a certain social group. The public may have found out about the crime from the newspapers, but there also may have been sources of scuttlebutt from within the OSS itself. Patten's letter suggests how titillating the news of the crime was to the people with whom Dahl and Rosemary associated.

> It was a dreadful thing, as they both worked in the O.S.S. and she was very attractive and much liked, and he had been pursuing her for months and she would have none of him. Finally one night he came to see her and her tactful girl friends left her alone with her beau and he proceeded to shoot her and then kill himself. I didn't know either of them, but everyone else in Washington seems to have and you can imagine the excitement caused locally.[8]

The event that provided grist for the Washington gossip mill was a catastrophe for two widely different families. It was also a potential setback for the OSS.

---

8 Jennet Conant, *The Irregulars: Roald Dahl and the British Spy Ring in Wartime Washington* (New York: Simon & Schuster, 2008), 171-2.

CHAPTER 24

THE AFTERMATH

The morning after the tragedy, July 13th, the police arrived on the doorstep of Margaret Chandler's cottage and broke the news: her husband was dead of a self-inflicted gunshot wound; before shooting himself he had used the same gun to murder a woman presumed to be his lover. The police also revealed to her that her husband's secret life included a rental apartment in downtown Washington.[1] In that one moment Margaret Chandler's life changed utterly. The shock waves from the tragedy spread outward, traumatizing his family, his friends, Rosemary's family, Elizabeth Maguire, and his colleagues at the OSS training schools.

Margaret Chandler faced not only the sudden loss of her husband and the income on which she and her two sons depended, but she also had to contend with the perception that he may have been involved with another woman. The newspapers heaped further humiliation on her by splashing that assumption across their pages.

Living with her sons in a cottage in rural Maryland where she had arrived only a few months earlier, Margaret was isolated from friends who might have given her emotional support. Her husband's aunt, Helen Knox, arrived to help, but no one from her own family came to stand by her side. Because her sons were sent elsewhere,

---

1 "Suitor Slays North Shore Heiress, Self," *Chicago Sun*, July 15, 1943. The building in the 1700 block of H Street no longer exists.

first for a brief stay with the Enders family and later for longer periods with her own family members in Texas and Arkansas, Margaret did not have the comfort of her children's presence. When W.K.'s personal effects were later returned to her, she found that her husband had not even opened some of the letters she had written to him. That discovery, in addition to what she had already suffered, must have been psychologically devastating.

Her financial situation was also dire. W.K. had left unpaid bills for dental work and for storing the family's furniture back in Nashville. Margaret would need financial support while recovering from the emotional effects of the tragedy and further down the line she would require job training to provide for herself and her children. Her cash assets amounted to $73.87; her sons each had a $50 war bond. She was, in short, alone and virtually penniless.

W.K.'s former colleagues at Vanderbilt, Harvard, and the University of Chicago wrote condolence letters describing him as a gifted and valuable human being. Along with tributes to his personal qualities came offers of financial aid from two professors at the University of Chicago.[2]

R. H. Griffith, a professor of eighteenth-century literature at the University of Texas and one of W.K.'s early

---

[2] All but one of the original condolence letters have disappeared. The quotations below come from excerpts from the letters typed by Helen Knox, W.K.'s aunt, who compiled the selections and sent carbon copies to family members. They are undated.

mentors, wrote that to have him "cut down early, before he had got done what he was capable of makes me feel as if a segment of what I was trying to accomplish had got broken up," adding that W. K. was "one of my men." Edwin Mims, retired chairman of the English department at Vanderbilt, wrote that "he was [as much] a victim of the war as any soldier shell-shocked on the battlefield...[he] was one of the most charming men I have ever met and one of the most scholarly." Mims also spoke of W. K.'s devotion to his family and his warm hospitality.

Walter C. Curry, the chairman of Vanderbilt's English department at the time of the tragedy, described W. K. as "an excellent scholar, an inspiring and sympathetic teacher, and a warm friend," adding that he "was a war casualty, strained to the breaking point by mysterious and unknown forces, overworked so that the bounds of his sensitive personality were tragically broken down." An unidentified student at Vanderbilt added that "the students were just killed...[he] was very popular both on the campus and in the classroom."

One of the most important letters came from Harold J. Coolidge, who had recruited W. K. for the OSS. Coolidge, a distinguished zoologist on leave from Harvard where he may have known W. K. during his years there as an instructor, enjoyed a reputation as a research scientist and later as an ecologist that extended well beyond academia. Coolidge's letter to Margaret Chandler suggests how impressed this eminent man was by W. K.'s character and abilities.

I was extremely fond of Knox and was closely associated with his office work for several months. He did an extremely good job and worked like a dynamo! I have seldom seen a man turn out results from original research in such a short time. Things finally reached a point where it was difficult to find enough to keep him busy and so he changed to another more responsible job. From then on I only saw him occasionally, but I heard high praise for the results which he was getting. Two Sundays ago I expected to spend the weekend with him when something unforeseen came up and changed his plans. [Margaret said that her husband had one of his severe headaches and did not feel equal to having a guest.] I very much want you to know of the high regard that I have for Knox and the splendid contribution which he made to his country's war effort up to the moment he lost his mind. Anyone is liable to crack from the special strains that they are put under in war conditions and Washington casualties are more numerous than authorities care to admit. While Knox died under highly tragic circumstances he left an inspiring record behind him of which you and your children and his

friends can be proud. He was an inspiring
fellow and will be greatly missed.

         With deepest sympathy,
         Harold J. Coolidge[3]

Coolidge, compassionate as well as brilliant, appealed to Whitney Shepardson, head of the OSS Secret Intelligence Branch, for financial aid for the widow. Theoretically it should have been possible. Because insurance companies refused to write policies for OSS agents whose names and job descriptions were top secret, Donovan had said that he would pay death benefits from his secret funds, but this assistance may have been intended only for agents killed in the field.[4] Because Coolidge saw W. K.'s death not as a crime but as a casualty of war caused by the pressures of his work, he thought the OSS might agree to compensate Margaret, as his memo to Shepardson suggests:

> If we assume that Chandler was completely
> mad at the time of his death, and there seems
> to be clear evidence for this assumption, an
> investigation of the work that he was
> doing for OSS would reveal that the
> nature of the job he was doing could have

---

3 Harold J. Coolidge to Margaret Chandler, not dated, but before August 20, 1943.

4 Douglas Waller, *Wild Bill Donovan*, 99.

and probably did contribute in no small measure to his state of mind. He was a very intense individual and threw himself wholeheartedly into everything that he undertook. He took very seriously his teaching assignment at the [F]arm and must have been unconsciously undermining his own mental balance by trying to solve the problems of his students. He had a very real responsibility from the point of view of the school security constantly weighing heavily on his mind. He had a real job with considerable difficulties in connection with running the school, the Farm, and the household at the Farm; all this in addition to any personal problems he may have had to cope with.

I hope that OSS will take immediate steps to somehow protect their men during the training period with insurance similar to that available to the army. If this is done the instructors should have the same protection, because their job is not without real danger especially from accident. Under such circumstances couldn't something be done on retroactive basis out of Special Funds to help the destitute Chandler widow and children? If nothing can be done the widow will have to pass the hat among personal friends to pay off his debts, and I understand the outlook is very black. He had many friends in academic circles and I think that OSS would be open to considerable public criticism, especially if through his wife or by some devious means outsiders could discover what his job had been.

I realize that what the OSS does for the widow becomes a matter of public record but I think that this situation could be "handled" and a settlement made which would stop all criticism and which could be justified if at any future time should there be an investigation of the use that was being made of Special Funds in this instance.

This whole matter has been so well handled up to the present time, that it would be unfortunate to fall down in the final stage, if any way could be found to lessen the effect of this tragedy in which OSS was indirectly involved.[5]

Coolidge's memo points out that the OSS wants to maintain secrecy and that paying the widow would be a public act,

---

5 Harold Coolidge to [Whitney] Shepardson, undated, National Archives, Knox Chandler (RG 226) A1224 230 86 28 05.

but thinks that this situation can be "handled" (Coolidge's quotes) as it has been up to the present moment. Although it is not clear from Coolidge's letter exactly how the OSS has "handled" the situation, so far at least everything has gone smoothly; the OSS as an organization has avoided negative publicity and W. K.'s role within the agency has remained a secret. But Coolidge points to the responsibility of the OSS in the suicide, the pressures weighing on W. K., and especially to his "real responsibility from the point of view of the school security constantly weighing heavily on his mind." To Coolidge, keeping secret the nature of the "Farm" was clearly of prime importance.

On July 22, 1943, Helen Knox wrote to the OSS also requesting financial assistance for Margaret, but the respondent reported that "there was no permissible way in which it [could] be done."[6] A little more than a week earlier, the OSS had sent her a $50 savings bond and a check for two weeks' back pay in the amount of $433.18 along with a form for the withheld tax and the writer's deepest sympathies.[7] The OSS also covered funeral expenses and transportation for the family and the body back to Brownwood. Aunt Helen, who escorted the coffin and traveled first-class, paid her own expenses. Donovan paid

---

6 J. R. MacMillan, to Helen Knox, July 26, 1943, National Archives, Knox Chandler (RG 226) 230 86 2 05 Box 117.

7 C[harles] J. Lennihan, Jr., to Margaret Chandler, July 14, 1943, National Archives, (RG 226) 230 86 2 05 Box 117.

nothing from the Special Funds, and Margaret received nothing more from the OSS.

⌣

The Sidley family made its own efforts to cope with Rosemary's death. A day or two after the murder Irene Sidley and her son-in-law Herbert H. Kennedy arrived from Chicago to claim Rosemary's body. Herbert H. Kennedy, married to Rosemary's younger sister Josephine, was a lawyer, educated at Princeton and Harvard Law School, and a veteran of World War I. Rosemary's father, Frank Chapman Sidley, was no longer living, so Herbert Kennedy was a reasonable choice to accompany Irene when she went to Washington to recover her daughter's body. The fact that he was a prominent lawyer certainly would have added weight to Irene's inquiries as to what had happened. But, according to the Sidley family, General Donovan himself told Irene the "real story" of Rosemary's death after which she and her son-in-law returned to Chicago, never demanding any further investigation of the tragedy and never revealing the secret of the "real story."

⌣

If the two deaths devastated the Chandler and Sidley families, they also threatened the secrecy of the OSS and its training schools, though the newspaper reports published around the time of the crime suggest that the agency itself managed to avoid the harsh glare of publicity. Although the early newspaper accounts state that both W. K. and Rosemary were employed by the OSS, they make no further mention of the spy organization. The stories say nothing about the "Farm," nothing about Chandler's role training men for espionage, and, above all, nothing about how the OSS was implicated in his death, which Coolidge suggested when he remarked that an investigation into the work W. K. was doing for the OSS would reveal that his job probably contributed to his emotional instability.

Silence began to surround W. K.'s death soon after the event. Within the Chandler family Helen Knox persuaded Margaret not to delve into the tragedy, since the bereaved widow was in no psychological state to do so. When Knox and Colston arrived at the Enders household in Swarthmore to stay for a few days while Margaret dealt with matters in Clinton, the Enders children (according to Trudy Enders) were cautioned not to mention W. K. to his sons. Margaret Chandler, believing that her husband killed himself and his stenographer because she resisted his advances, began working to put the past behind her, preparing for the future by studying for a degree in social work. Carrie Chandler did not talk about the tragedy, at least to Knox and me. As far as I can discover Margaret never willingly spoke of her husband, certainly not to me. Knox, in retrospect, wondered how it never occurred to him to ask his mother about his father, but he never did. The silence around the tragedy would remain unbroken for more than four decades.

CHAPTER 25
THE MYSTERY

When I told Knox in 1984 that his father had killed a woman before he committed suicide, I told him only what the *Chicago Sun* had told me, that W. K. Chandler murdered Rosemary Sidley because she had rejected his advances. After Knox and I concluded our puzzling interview with Dr. Robert Enders, I was not at all certain that what I thought was true was indeed the case. Then, in 2004, when I learned through the *OSS Society Journal* that the Sidley family thought that General Donovan had personally told Irene Sidley the "real story," I was finally galvanized to try to discover what had really happened.

Knox and I had both been troubled by the way Enders had staged the interview, not allowing us to ask questions and telling us only what he wanted us to know. We were also confused because he contradicted things in the newspaper stories: that the relationship between Rosemary and W. K. was "platonic" (although he also claimed that he had burned the "love letters"), that he arrived at the crime scene almost immediately, that the bodies were on the patio, and that W. K. had not been in an auto accident a few weeks before the killings. Most disturbing was his assertion that he had "told the newspapers what to say." Was he telling the truth to us in 1984? Or had he told the truth to the newspapers in 1943?

Years later, when Knox and I looked back on the interview, we recognized Enders as a man who expected to control events, a man capable of indirection and artifice (as his daughter Trudy later confirmed). His obituary in the *Swarthmore College Bulletin* hints at this, describing his teaching style as "lectures of subtle elegance [with] searching and stimulating questions that led his pupils to delve and develop their own resources."[1] A former student recalled him as her "most Socratic, enigmatic, unconventional, crusty non-performer 'you-have-to-learn-it-yourself' professor."[2] I believe he treated Knox and me the way he had approached his students, planting the seed that a "real" story existed and leaving it to us to unearth that story. Enders, then in his mid-80s, might also have wanted Knox, the son of his former colleague, to discover that the tragedy was something other than an ill-fated love affair.

We also wondered how Enders had gotten to the crime scene so quickly if Elizabeth Maguire had shouted out the window for help, as she claimed. She was in the bathtub. She had heard shots and a scream. She had no idea whether the shooter was still alive and could shoot again. Knowing what I later discovered about her fear of going downstairs, it seemed reasonable that she would

---

1 Robert C. Wallach, *Swarthmore College Bulletin*, January 26, 1988.

2 Phyllis Wise, '67, "Swarthmore College Past Commencements," http://www.swarthmore.edu/past-commencements/phyllis-wise-67.

have shouted out the window. But since she was employed by the OSS, had she also telephoned the agency about the shooting? If she had, Enders might have told her what to say to the police just as he had instructed the reporters what to say.

But even though the meeting with Enders muddied my understanding of events, two things became very clear to me. The first was that the OSS had created a cover-up to distract attention from itself. The second was that W. K. Chandler's mental health had deteriorated severely by the time of his death.

—

First, I believe that the OSS cover-up began with the newspapers, which reported on the tragedy the day after it happened and followed up the story for several days, honing in on W. K.'s status as a rejected suitor or a jealous lover. The agency could not prevent the deaths from being publicly known since the police had arrived soon after the shooting and the reporters shortly after them. But if the OSS could not stop the newspapers from printing the story, at least the agency could exercise "damage control," putting a spin on events that worked to their favor.

Enders, who claimed he had told the newspapers what to say, could have offered the reporters the gossipy, almost irresistible story of a rejected lover who murdered the woman he loved because, according to the *Chicago*

Sun, "he couldn't bear to live without her."[3] Enders may also have told Elizabeth Maguire to say that she had overheard a jealous argument between W. K. and Rosemary before the fatal shots, as some of the newspaper accounts reported. I find it difficult to believe that W. K., who had led an ordered existence as a scholar and a family man, who had been chosen as chief instructor of the elite Secret Intelligence Training School, would murder a woman because she rejected him romantically.

While the reporters energetically followed up the sensational aspects of the case, they said little about the OSS. The first article that came out, in the *Washington Post* on July 13, mentioned only that W. K. and Rosemary were both employed by the OSS. The *Post* later reported that W. K. was her supervisor. Rosemary was identified either as a "government stenographer" or as a "clerical worker," terms used to describe most of the women who worked for the OSS whatever their actual responsibilities. Nothing appeared in print about the "Farm," no details about the work that W. K. performed there.

General Donovan himself might have orchestrated the cover-up, assigning Enders to mislead the newspapers and then meeting in person with Irene Sidley, using his power and prestige to convince her not to investigate Rosemary's death. Since Donovan was accountable only to FDR, he controlled both the content and flow of information; he could destroy or classify as he saw fit, leaving

---

3 "Suitor Slays North Shore Heiress, Self," *Chicago Sun*, July 15, 1943.

no paper trail of his conversation with Mrs. Sidley. What he said could have been true or false, but the fact that Donovan approached her at all suggests the importance of hiding something from the public, of preventing any possible outside inquiry. Mrs. Sidley did what he wanted; according to her family she remained silent to the end of her life about the content of their conversation, taking her secret to her grave.

A second indication that the OSS was covering up the details of the tragedy occurs, by inference, in the memo in which Harold Coolidge, W. K.'s friend, mentor, and recruiter, attempted to convince the OSS to assist the widowed Margaret Chandler financially. Coolidge does not directly mention the tragedy, but he alludes to it.[4] He points out the importance of remaining quiet about any additional payment to Margaret because the OSS "would be open to considerable public criticism, especially if through his wife or by some devious means outsiders could discover what his job had been." So far, says Coolidge, the OSS has managed the matter so well that it would be unfortunate to bungle it in the final stage. Coolidge does not explain how the OSS has handled the matter, but he does emphasize the need to keep the training school out of the public eye. Certainly the OSS wanted the "Farm" to remain top secret, misrepresenting the spy school to its Maryland neighbors as a test site for new military "gadgets."

---

4 For Coolidge's memo, see Chapter 24, The Aftermath, pages 383-386

The reasons the OSS needed to stifle or spin publicity seem obvious. The OSS was a clandestine organization; it dealt in secrets, underhanded tricks, and subversion; silence regarding its projects was essential to national security. Beyond that, there were political reasons for a cover-up. From the moment it was created, the OSS had drawn the anger of competing intelligence organizations in the army, navy, and state department. J. Edgar Hoover was especially jealous of Donovan, of Donovan's closeness to FDR, and of the OSS in general, which he saw as muscling in on FBI territory. Donovan's enemies looked for any opportunity to attack and would have taken advantage of any opening to smear the reputation of the OSS.

Furthermore, some of Donovan's initiatives would have given his enemies plenty of ammunition even in a wartime atmosphere where many things were permitted. One of these troubling projects was experimentation with a "truth drug" (TD). Stanley P. Lovell, whom Donovan had hired in 1942 to try out "subtle devices and underhanded tricks" for use against the enemy, pointed out in his memoir that the "schools and recruiting people" needed a truth drug to help "screen out German spies or sympathizers." The prisoner-of-war officers in the military also sought such a drug to use in interrogating prisoners.[5]

---

5 Stanley P. Lovell, *Of Spies & Stratagems* (Englewood Cliffs, NJ: Prentice-Hall, 1963), 57.

Lovell's scientists tested their potential truth drugs on unsuspecting human subjects, among them soldiers who believed they were participating in research to develop treatments for shell shock.[6] Another unwitting human guinea pig was a New York gangster, August Del Gaizo, known on the street as Little Augie. While under the influence of a potential truth drug, a cigarette laced with a marijuana-related compound, he bragged about his successes at bribery and opium smuggling, but he was never formally accused of these crimes because the research in TD as well as the OSS's explorations of chemical and biological warfare, had to remain secret.

The OSS, then, was vulnerable if knowledge about its ventures into mind-altering drugs became public, especially since the Geneva Conventions had placed limitations on techniques for questioning prisoners of war.[7] A congressional investigation was the last thing Donovan needed.

～

While Coolidge's memo and Enders' statement that he had "told the newspapers what to say" suggested to me an OSS cover-up, the fact that I could find only one OSS official document stating that W. K. Chandler had killed Rosemary

---

6 Waller, *Wild Bill Donovan*, 103.

7 Lovell, *Spies & Stratagems*, 57.

Sidley reinforced my suspicion. The OSS personnel files that I retrieved from the National Archives contain records of financial settlements (to Margaret Chandler and Irene Sidley) and of personal efforts to help the Chandler family, but have no further information about the deaths. The minutes of the Executive Committee of the OSS also remain strangely silent about an event publicized in newspapers nationwide.

The only OSS document I could find that does mention the murder and suicide is *The History of the Schools and Training Branch*, dating from late August 1945 and, according to the author, intended for use by general historians and specialists studying the history of American intelligence. Perhaps both its timing as the war drew to a close and its purpose as a research tool prevented its being redacted. The probable author is Kenneth P. Miller, who in June 1943 was acting chief of the Schools and Training Branch. Two years later, by then promoted to major, he headed the intelligence section of the Schools and Training headquarters, which, he remarked "risked its professional reputation by undertaking the writing of this Branch history." [8] The book describes the difficulties faced by the schools, including their frequent re-organizations, some only months apart, as the agency struggled to set up an efficient hierarchy of command. The haste and confusion caused by the need to accomplish a lot in a short time in the Schools & Training Branch, Miller notes, "reflects

---

8 *History of the Schools and Training Branch*, 160.

the history of the OSS in general, because the same overall policy that dictated a tremendous drive for speed, mass production and mass results, at times gave the OSS an impression of hopeless confusion and indecisive direction."[9]

For purposes of my research Miller's discussion stands out because he not only acknowledges W. K.'s death but points out that it negatively affected Schools and Training:

> Knox Chandler, an ex-newspaperman and college teacher, had shown signs of being somewhat neurotic at the time he was recruited by Col. Baker. But to look ahead and foresee the result of this neurosis is surely asking too much of Baker who only saw a big man with ability and great energy at a time when he desperately needed such a man. Three weeks before Chandler killed himself and Miss Rosemary Sidley [Miss Rosemary Sidley and himself] he had been involved in an auto accident. His head was badly lacerated, and he suffered some shock, but he insisted upon carrying on his part of the program at RTU11 [the "Farm"] because the size of classes was increasing. The accident probably did not

---

9 *History of the Schools and Training Branch*, 3.

directly precipitate the tragedy, although it
was probably [a] contributing factor. Like
the innocent bystander who is always shot
in such affairs, the Schools and Training
Branch suffered from this event.[10]

Though Miller doesn't discuss precisely how
Schools and Training suffered "like the innocent
bystander," the Chronology that precedes and summarizes
the text of the *History* does offer hints. The Chronology
mentions W. K. Chandler's death "and the implications
thereof" as one of two significant events in July 1943. The
other is the "first of a number of investigations angled
toward reorganization of S&T."[11] The chronological
notes for August and September remark on continued
investigations, with re-assignment of personnel and the
arrival and departure of a new executive for Schools
and Training. The entry for January 1944 mentions the
opening of the "First Assessment Station… additional
staff of psychologists and psychiatrists from Harvard," the
beginning of the attempt to select men who could tolerate
the pressures of their wartime assignments. The *History*,
then, makes it clear that W. K.'s death was an important
event affecting the Schools and that it resulted in at least
one internal investigation. Whatever organizational

---

10 *History of the Schools and Training Branch*, 63.

11 *History of the Schools and Training Branch*, 7.

changes and inquiries the tragedy triggered, however, must have taken place within the organization, without attracting outside notice.

——

My second certainty, after realizing that the OSS had created a cover-up, was that in July 1943, W. K. Chandler's mental health was precarious. Miller describes W. K. as already "somewhat neurotic" when he moved from Research and Analysis to the "Farm" as chief instructor; he further sees the tragedy as "the result of this neurosis." Even long before the tragedy, W. K.'s friends and colleagues had described him as "sensitive" and "intense," suggesting he might not stand up well to the increasing pressures of his job.[12] He may have been too sensitive for the brutal training in hand-to-hand combat he had received and too morally uncompromising to accept some of the devious uses of drugs that were part of the OSS's stock in trade. Enders had noted that W. K. could not accept the idea that anything was allowable during wartime.

As the pressures of W. K.'s job increased, his fragile emotional state expressed itself in his inability to sleep (reported by his wife), his daytime drinking (reported

---

12 As I have mentioned, Harold Coolidge called him "a very intense individual" who "threw himself wholeheartedly into everything that he undertook." Walter C. Curry, chair of the Vanderbilt English department, who had known him before the war, described him as having a "sensitive personality."

by Enders), and possibly the severe headache that had prevented Harold Coolidge from visiting two Sundays before the tragedy.

According to Miller, the auto accident, whose existence Enders denied, may also have been a factor. But despite W. K.'s injuries and his emotional "shock," he insisted on returning to his duty, because "the size of his classes was increasing," an indication of the man's sense of responsibility and patriotism. W. K.'s need to maintain the security of the school was, according to Harold Coolidge, a further constant source of stress.

A final indication of W. K.'s deteriorating mental health is the letter he wrote to Rosemary.[13] Although the newspapers offered it as evidence of his jealous love for his assistant, for me it provided additional evidence of W. K.'s emotional instability. The letter is the only personal document written by W. K. that survives (the others are academic papers), and it is the most revealing, showing his intelligence and his facility with words, but also his frayed emotional state. Like our interview with Enders, it raises more questions than it answers, questions about its authorship, the date of composition, and the way the police got hold of it.

Since no handwritten or signed typed version exists, we cannot be absolutely certain that W. K. himself wrote it, although the style is sophisticated, educated, and polished, the kind of writing we might expect from

13 For the full text of the letter, see Chapter 23, pages 285-288

someone who made his living reading and writing. Furthermore, the obscure joke about Byron and Coleridge suggests that the letter's author knew a great deal about the history of English literature.

Although the letter as quoted by the *Washington Post* is undated, it was probably written around June of 1943, because W. K. mentions his love for Rosemary as having guided him for six months. Her employment records show that she took the oath of office in August 1942, when she was described as a clerk-stenographer. W. K. probably met her around January 1943, when he moved to the "Farm." By April of that year she had been promoted to junior administrative assistant and in June she became his own administrative assistant.

Finally, how did the newspaper get the letter? The *Washington Post* on July 14, reported that a detective sergeant had found two letters from W. K. in Rosemary's belongings, letters that protested his love for her. The following day, July 15, the *Post* reported that "a single one of Chandler's letters" was given to the press, the letter that the *Post* printed in full. There is no mention of what happened to the other letter mentioned the previous day. Also on July 15, the *Chicago Daily Tribune*, in a "special" to that paper, refers to the letter as well as "many interoffice memos" from W. K. to Rosemary, which no other source mentions. It is possible that Enders provided the love letter to the police, or allowed it to be found among Rosemary's belongings, as part of his role in controlling information about the tragedy. After all, he told Knox and me that he had burned the "love letters," implying that at some time he was in possession of correspondence between W. K. and Rosemary.

—

W. K. begins his letter to Rosemary by thanking her for letting him take her to lunch, something she seems not to have wanted to do, since she did him a favor by going. The lunch conversation must have gone well, since he claims he can sleep that night knowing that she will forgive him. But forgive him for what? He has, he admits, said and done "horrid" things out of anger, he has lost his self-control, but we have no way of knowing what he said or did.

Although W. K. acknowledges that he is writing a love letter, "the first I have ever written you wholly as such," he does not mention any of Rosemary's physical attributes, her beauty, or her desirability; nor does anything in the letter suggest that she and W. K. have kissed, embraced, or been in any way sexually intimate. Instead of describing her physical charms, he itemizes the personal qualities that have brought him to love her: her honesty, loyalty, intelligence, wit, and charm, all of them woven together "in the rich and lovable fabric" that is her personality. That last phrase is strange, formal and even awkward, but perhaps his academic side is expressing itself. Enders had insisted that the relationship between the two was "platonic," and it may well have been in the sense that he thought W. K. and Rosemary were not sexually involved, but the tone of the letter is passionate, and W. K. is describing here something more than an ordinary office friendship.

A second theme of the letter is uncertainty, a "flaming hell" of uncertainty, a "nightmare," an "abnormality" that has robbed him of his peace and emotional control. Once that uncertainty is resolved he is sure that his confidence in her abilities and her work will be restored. We cannot tell the exact nature of the uncertainty; it might be uncertainty in her affection for him, since he speaks of his jealousy, but his term "abnormality" does not suggest jealousy of another man. Nor does the letter express disappointment that any affection she may have had for him has cooled. It simply harps on the "uncertainty," the "abnormality," the "nightmare." It occurred to me that this "abnormality" or "uncertainty" and the subsequent deaths of W. K. and Rosemary might have resulted from something in their professional relationship as colleagues in the secret intelligence agency. But whatever the "abnormality" or "uncertainty," the letter makes it clear that W. K. is a man at his wits' end, a man whose sanity is unraveling.

⌣

If W. K. had lost his sanity by the summer of 1943, if he remained convinced that some OSS tactics were morally unacceptable (as Enders maintained), he may have become a liability to the organization. If he knew about the OSS programs to develop a truth drug or Donovan's interest in chemical and biological warfare, he may have been troubled by efforts at mind control or weapons that slaughtered civilians. Perhaps he even indicated displeasure with directions that OSS research was taking. Although I have not found any evidence, it is possible that W. K. and other OSS members were, like the army subjects and the gangster "Little Augie," given truth drugs without knowing it.

In my attempts to understand the mystery of his death, I have sometimes wondered whether W. K.'s superiors in the agency, recognizing his instability, could no longer trust him to keep its secrets. This scenario like the others I have developed raises unanswerable questions.

Although post-traumatic stress disorder was not recognized by that name until after the war in Vietnam, the devastating psychological effects of war have long been recognized. The symptoms W. K. showed during his last days at the "Farm" were among those that would later be associated with PTSD: sleeplessness, angry outbursts (i.e. saying or doing "horrid things"), feelings of guilt or blame ("little peace and at times no control"). Harold Coolidge spoke of him as "completely mad" at the time of his death, an assumption for which there was "clear evidence." When Coolidge spoke in his memo about the OSS having a role indirectly in W. K.'s death, he acknowledged that the chief instructor at the "Farm" was placed in a position he could not cope with and was left there without support.[14]

One of his former colleagues at Vanderbilt pointed out in a condolence letter that W. K. "was [as much] a victim of the war as any soldier shell-shocked on the battlefield." But as a civilian member of the OSS, W. K. did not enjoy the rights and privileges of soldiers who died on the battlefield. Instead his memory was sacrificed so that the agency for which he worked could continue unperturbed in its mission. He did not get a military funeral with an honor guard and the presentation of a flag. But I have often thought that, at the cemetery in Brownwood, his colleagues in the training schools and the professors from the universities where he taught should have stood at attention alongside his friends and his family from Texas.

And there should have been a bugler sounding the mournful notes of Taps. It would have been a ceremony that no one, especially his son Pachy, would have forgotten. Instead, when Margaret Chandler buried the body of her husband, she hoped also to bury the things about his life that she considered shameful secrets. In doing so, she imposed on those around her a silence that almost obliterated his memory altogether.

---

14 After W. K.'S death, the agency undertook a major reorganization of the training schools and started a program for psychologically screening candidates.

EPILOGUE

This memoir tells the story of my life as a daughter, a wife, a mother, and an artist. It also reconstructs to the best of my ability the story of W. K. Chandler, which was shrouded in silence. As I worked, I discovered that the two threads of my memoir are linked by my understanding of the destructive nature of silence.

My childhood was tainted by my mother's alcoholism and the need to keep it secret from outsiders. My relationship with my mother-in-law was strained by Margaret's refusal to talk about her husband. Her threatening body language and angry outbursts effectively silenced me for decades and drew me into the conspiracy as I kept the secret from Knox. Margaret's silence also affected her relationships with friends, family, and the people of Brownwood who never spoke to Knox and Colston about their father's death.

Part of my motive for writing this memoir, then, is to free W. K. from the silence Margaret created. I think I have succeeded in painting a portrait of him as a good son, a gifted teacher, a warm and humorous human being, a brilliant scholar, and a patriot. Undoubtedly his tragic breakdown came about because he was unbearably tormented by the stresses of his position as chief instructor in the OSS Secret Intelligence Training School. I hope my readers will understand that he was as much a casualty of war as the men and women killed in combat. I also hope that my children and grandchildren, reading this, will come to cherish W. K. Chandler's memory.

I am disappointed that I could not pin down the exact truth of what happened on the evening of July 12, 1943, in Rosemary Sidley's house in Georgetown, but I have come to terms with uncertainty and can accept that I will probably never know exactly what happened. I have come to understand that the silences in my own family and in my husband's were small-scale compared to the conspiracy the OSS constructed. Our secrets were personal and tacit; the ones required of OSS recruits were institutional and explicit, justifiable because the country was at war and the OSS had to protect its wartime strategies. I think that Bob Enders was evasive about the tragedy because he continued keeping his oath of secrecy decades after the war had ended. I think that people higher in the OSS bureaucracy than Bob Enders conspired to remove almost all evidence from their files concerning W. K. Chandler's job at the agency and ultimately the cause of his death. I think that General Donovan told Irene Sidley something that made her drop her inquiries into Rosemary's death.

In the process of writing this memoir, I have learned a great deal about myself. I have survived not being the beautiful second child my mother hoped for or the socially prominent Southern belle and doctor's wife she wanted me to become. I coped with raising four children born within seven years and with the responsibility of caring for them on a very modest income while my husband pursued his career in science. I coped with being repeatedly uprooted, moving into and out of many houses before our family settled into North Guilford. After years of effort, sometimes sidelined by distractions, I reached the point where I could confidently call myself an artist, producing work that has satisfied me and attracted attention beyond my immediate circle. I learned to speak out, after having felt for years that I had to protect the secrets of my mother and my mother-in-law. I have learned to appreciate my mother-in-law's struggle and the toll her secret must have taken on her.

I have also come to understand that secrecy raises emotional barriers within families and that the silences of one generation are passed down to the next. My husband Knox suffered from losing his father and was unable to talk about it. Carrie Chandler, W. K.'s mother, could not openly express her grief on the loss of her son, especially after Margaret came to live with her. As long as I remained silent about W. K.'s death, I too suffered because I could not confide in my husband. Knox and Knox Jr. never had the close relationship that they might have had if Knox had come to terms with his own childhood loss.

Seeley Chandler put it best when she remarked that W. K.'s death was "like a nuclear bomb in a way, a complete disaster in the center but affecting people at great distance, too," a disaster made worse by the secrecy surrounding it.

⌣

In 2010, Knox retired from a successful career in scientific research, internationally recognized for his achievements. In retirement he renewed his interest in "reading" physics, a subject that had fascinated him from his undergraduate days. As he and I worked together on this memoir, he began to recover memories that he had lost during the years when his father was a forbidden topic.

The love that Knox and I felt for one another endured and strengthened as we looked forward to our 60th wedding anniversary. We looked back on our lives, filled with gratitude for our careers and for having been able to raise our children in the country home we both loved, seeing our grandchildren run through the same fields their parents had enjoyed as youngsters. We planned to spend our last days overlooking these meadows, which came to signify the continuity of our lives, as we looked forward to more summer visits on the screened-in porch, with opportunities to reminisce about the past and share plans for the future.

Sadly these plans came to an abrupt end on March 20, 2017, when Knox died from a hemorrhagic stroke, a severe shock for me and our family. He lived only five days from the onset of the brain bleed. We Chandlers, as well as his many friends and colleagues, sorely miss his intelligence, dry wit, kindness, generosity of spirit, and his presence, which brought lightness into our lives.

The first seven grandchildren in Knox's wildflower meadow, 1997
All nine grandchildren on front porch, 2018